SATURDAY'S CHILD

SATURDAY'S CHILD

Margaret Morris
as told to
Laura Ames

Cover design by
Alan Maravilla

iUniverse, Inc.
Bloomington

SATURDAY'S CHILD

Margaret Jean Morris
405 Fillmore Street
Taft, CA 93268

Laura Lee Ames
325 Fresno Street
Coalinga, CA 93210

Names, dates, and places have been changed to provide anonymity.

iUniverse books may be ordered through booksellers or by contacting:

iUniverse
1663 Liberty Drive
Bloomington, IN 47403
www.iuniverse.com
1-800-Authors (1-800-288-4677)

ISBN: 978-1-4759-6413-4 (sc)
ISBN: 978-1-4759-6414-1 (ebk)

Printed in the United States of America

iUniverse rev. date: 1/10/2013

Prologue: Susan Amon, M.A., M.F.C.C.
Epilogue: Joan C. Franz, M.S., M.F.C.C.

CONTENTS

Prologue...ix

Prelude To A Process xiii

The Secret...xix

Works Cited in the Secret.. xxv

Angie's Shame: A Study In Futility xxix

Part I
An Emotionally Decapitating Hell

Beginning: The Painful Road To Sanity............................... 3

The Journey Begins.. 5

Behind The Façade.. 10

The Players: As Cookie Knew Them 14

Suck In The Anger, Hide The Memories 22

Inside Out: Outside In 31

Isolation 40

Beyond Hell 53

The Void 59

Childhood Passes Into The Labyrinth Of Despair 68

The Sexual Abuse Ends Abruptly 78

Transference 83

Part II
Past and Present Collide

Hope Wanes 91
There Are No Fairy Tales 96
The Deceit Of Hope 103
The Resurrection Of Father's Control 111
Infirmities Of Mind, Body And Soul:
      A Family's Legacy 118
Road Blocks, Dead Ends, And Locked Doors 125
The End And . . . The Beginning 135

Part III
Cleaning Up the Cluttered Road to Sanity

My Quest For A Safe House Begins 147
To Father: May He Rest In Peace 150
The First Step 159
Obstacles: Self-Imposed 169
Obstacles: Familial 182
Open Letters To My Mom—And Myself 192
Epilogue 195
Addendum 197
Postscript 199

Works Cited 201
Author Bio 203

Dedicated to my husband Charles who put up with a lot
while Lollie and I worked on this story.
I know his patience wore thin, at times, especially when my
entire focus was getting Saturday's Child completed before
the end of the last century.
We didn't quite make it, but we are finished.
Done. Thank God!
Thank you, Charles, for hanging in there with me.

Quoted in "Miser Farebrother" by B.L. Farejean, *Harper's Weekly*, September 17,1887. Author Unknown

The child who is born on the Sabbath day
Is brave and bonny, and good and gay.
Monday's child is fair of face,
Tuesday's child is full of grace,
Wednesday's child is loving and giving,
Thursday's child works hard for a living,
Friday's child is full of woe,

But, Saturday's Child has far to go.

*Purposely placed out of order for emphasis. Original quote has Sabbath line last.

Prologue

I first met Jean when she, her husband, and their daughter Kay, came to me for help in resolving a family conflict. As often happens in therapy, another situation presents itself as the primary problem when a more serious problem is underlying. This, I believe, was the situation with Jean and her family. Kay and Jean had been having conflicts for quite a number of years. It appeared that they were having difficulty separating and it was time for Kay to become more independent. Jean verbalized that she was ready to have her daughter live on her own and that she and her husband were willing to financially support the move. Kay needed a slight push. The family organized the move with relative ease, and Kay and Jean managed the separation with minor strain. Jean was firm and Kay eventually began spending more and more time without the aid of her family.

After her daughter had been on her own for a month or so, Jean came back in to see me, this time for herself. With Kay well on her way, Jean was ready to confront the issues in her past that were holding her back from living a fully productive existence. Jean knew she had to take the plunge.

When I first met Jean, I was struck by her courage and determination. (I continue to admire her for these qualities.) In spite of her fears, Jean was willing to go the limit to come to terms with her past. Jean had good reasons to be afraid of pursuing the therapy. She was from a well-known family in a small town, and she had lived there most of her life. Jean had married and raised her family in the area.

Jean was 46 years old when she started to come to terms with the sexual abuse her father perpetrated on her as a child, and the physical abuse she had endured from both her parents. Jean's parents, brothers and sister lived close to her in this small town. They made it quite clear to her that they did not want Jean to reveal the family secrets. Of course, they denied that any abuse had occurred which made it twice as difficult for Jean to pursue her convictions. But then, Jean had courage and determination and she was *angry*.

Jean's defenses against the overwhelming feelings of anger over the years were anxiety and fear. She often came to each of our sessions anxious. I worked with her to become aware of the anger that was masked as fear and to give her permission to tell about and express that anger. Much of our time together was spent talking about anger and allowing her to express the anger toward her father and mother in safe ways. We did a lot of role-playing and *empty chair* work where Jean would place the image of her father or mother in a chair opposite her and express her feelings directly toward that person. Jean also began a journal in which she wrote her thoughts and feelings, thus getting them outside of herself where they could serve her better. Jean began to be more comfortable with her feelings of rage and became less afraid in the world.

As we confronted the feelings, we confronted the memories of the molest. New ones would come to her over time. With each new memory we worked gently through the hurt, rage, fear and shame. Along with Jean's new awareness of her feelings, I taught her about the *inner child*. She remembered that she had been called *Cookie* as a child. *Cookie* now took a front seat and for several sessions we talked about how to nurture *Cookie* and heal her wounds. Jean took hold of the inner child concept quickly.

She began coming to sessions with a comforting friend, a stuffed animal. I had Jean find pictures of herself as a child—ones that she liked. I taught her how to do the *mirror exercise* where she would say kind, loving and nurturing things to her mirror image each morning.

Jean continued to empower herself with these exercises and her depression and anxiety gradually lifted. Her strength increased and she was able to confront her parents with their continual cover-up and denial of the truth. Through the tears, fears, rage and fists, Jean began to forgive herself and take risks to expand her life.

Jean had never learned to drive a car and she determined to get her driver's license, which she did. When she became more assertive with her husband, she reported that their relationship was improving. She talked of going to school to get a college degree. She remained outspoken with friends and demanded the truth from others.

Jean remained in therapy with me until I had to leave. We discussed her continuing in therapy with a Women's Group. I felt it was time that Jean avail herself of the support that can only come from a group of women who are dealing with the same personal issue of molest. Though afraid, Jean took *Cookie* gently by the hand and led her to the Group where she continues to grow and learn. In my short time with Jean, I learned a whole new lesson in courage and conviction. I felt honored, as I often do with clients, to be able to share in Jean's journey.

"Thank you, Jean, for the privilege of knowing you. You continue to be an inspiration to the ones whose lives you have touched."

Susan L. Amon, M.A., M.F.C.C.
February 1992

PRELUDE TO A PROCESS

L.L. Ames

There were three reasons I befriended Jean: 1) She was intelligent; 2) she was sad; and 3) she peaked my curiosity.

I am not certain what Jean did when I first met her that led me to believe she was intelligent. Perhaps it was her language, her analytical insight into others with whom we found ourselves participating, or the way she dealt with her children. Too many years have passed to remember specifics, but I do recall that my initial assessment was quickly made and I have never, in the 19 years of our acquaintance, questioned my first impression.

I can, however, as I look back into our shared past, envision her sadness with absolute clarity for she wore it like a badge of courage, almost daring anyone to take it from her. The sadness surrounded her every action and reaction, with a vehemence most men of battle pray for at their point of confrontation with an enemy. That was Jean. To her, every person was an automatic enemy to be wary of, mistrusted, and feared. She had great difficulty making friends because of her mistrust. The protective emotional cover she wrapped around herself was as if made of steel—impenetrable, unbending, solidly obstructing any view into the inner being. She was not open to a friendship with me at first, but I am a student and champion of human nature, and knew instinctively that Jean needed a soul-mate, a confidante—a friend. She could not rid herself of me, and I have never asked her if she tried because it would not have made a difference. I was a defender of the downtrodden and I was untiring in my efforts to establish a sense of trust in Jean, from Jean.

Before I met Jean, I had never known anyone who did not smile. Or rarely so. I had never known a person who never displayed a sense of humor or an ability to laugh at herself and life's foibles. Jean was so damned serious. Even some of the stodgy professors I had met in college didn't have the stoic demeanor of Jean. The more I was in her company, as a parent volunteer where our children attended school, the more curious I became. It was obvious to me that her sadness had created a barrier through which no more hurt could penetrate, and I was determined to break through that barrier and find out why Jean was the way she was.

As Jean and I began to share time outside the school environment, we became closer. Although she did not allow herself to entrust me with her innermost feelings, she did allow me partial entrance into her world of home and family. Her children were a delight to me and I enjoyed the times I spent in her home.

When she began to laugh at my silliness, I felt it a major breakthrough for Jean. Outside her house, she was reticent and serious to the point of appearing stuck-up to some of the other mothers who volunteered at the school. Inroads were being paved in our relationship, and one day I gathered the courage to ask her if she had been mistreated as a child. The barrier around Jean crumbled. I was surprised. "The only way many victims can survive their early incest traumas is to mount a psychological cover-up, pushing these memories so far beneath conscious awareness that they may not surface for years, if ever" (Forward 152).

Shortly after Jean's disclosure of the past she had suppressed for so long, my husband was transferred to another town. It was lousy timing, but we continued our friendship long distance. When Jean finally decided to get counseling for what was impeding her emotional progress, I was one of the first to know. I was also one of the first to applaud her decision. I knew she wouldn't receive support from her family, as abusive families wither because of their lies of perfect family, perfect children, no problems, Church-going, *Bible*-toting, "we're OK, everyone else is crazy," spewing from the lips of people who had emotionally and spiritually died, years before their bodies were to be placed in the ground.

Okay. *The Secret* was out. What happened from that point on would be up to Jean with the aid of a therapist, a supportive husband, and a friend willing to help by listening to tears and fears and frustration and anger—via the phone company.

Jean's therapist suggested that she put her past on paper, as a catharsis. Jean and I jointly agreed that putting all those words into book form would not only be cathartic, but just might help others with the same problems, and the same kinds of family secrets. Thus, this book was born.

It is now 2011, many years after her therapy which concluded in 1995. I have witnessed a miracle in this person named Jean. She is able to laugh and enjoy a funny incident or joke, she can face herself in the mirror with self-confidence and a sense of progress, and she confronts obstacles instead of barricading herself from them, or circumventing them. In learning that she is worthy she has found worth. Anger or hate no longer consume her and she demonstrates an amazing ability to love those who harmed her because she has learned and understands that our pasts may dictate our present, and that many people cause suffering because they, too, suffered as children.

As I've watched Jean emerge from behind her insulated, impenetrable wall of silence, I've experienced a sense of completion from my point of view. I like to think that I played a small role in the emancipation of Jean, whose inner self gets stronger with each passing month of therapy and self-awareness.

Jean's journey is ongoing. Her road to complete mental health is still strewn with bits of garbage here and there. More than fifty years of secrecy, shame and self-inflicted guilt do not leave one's mind easily—without emotional pain so deep it takes on a physical entity. Jean knows this and doesn't allow it to encapsulate her as she once did. She is willing to accept the challenge of whatever or whomever necessary for her continued emotional growth. She is learning that she need not share the family's guilt, nor be a part of the games they continue to play for the outside world.

Jean and I discussed at great length whether or not we should use the correct names of the family members in this manuscript. We decided against it, but not out of fear of retribution. To expose these people by name for the part they played would be of little value. What is past cannot be altered nor can we force members of her family to purge their own pain. That must be an individual's decision for it cannot be beneficial otherwise.

The purpose of this book, other than as a catharsis, is to help people who have experienced the same horror. There is hope and there is help in the form of therapists and support systems. It is important that individuals from abusive families realize that The Secret must be exposed in order for them to lead lives that are emotionally healthy, physically well, and intellectually productive.

Before we begin Jean's story, we would like to share "*The Secret*" and "Angie's Shame." These two chronicles are about women who suffered the plight of the sexually abused whose outcomes differ greatly because one demanded help and received it, the other wanted help but gave up when no one (including psychiatrists and family members) regarded her dysfunction, though being sexual in nature, as some sort of craziness peculiar to her alone.

Our intention is to give the reader insight into the fact that this sad, sick behavior affects too many for too long, and that it is Okay to expose the past and the people who took part. That in order to preserve one's own sanity, to regain the ability to give and accept love in a healthy relationship, and to grow into a person without hate and anger as the driving force of one's existence, it is imperative not only to seek help, but to insist upon receiving it.

Laura Lee Ames
Co-author and friend

THE SECRET

Leah White

According to Margaret Hyde in *Cry Softly! The Story of Child Abuse*, unknown numbers of children cry softly each day to hide the pain caused by child abuse (7). Some do not cry at all out of fear that terrible things will happen to them. These are the victims of sexual abuse who are the major keepers of *The Secret*.

I was asked to contribute to this preface because of my *secret*. For me it is an honor to do so as it means that more and more of us hidden victims are coming forward to expose the shame, guilt and degradation of a sexually abusive childhood. I will discuss, much from my own experience, some of the reasons why children as well as adults keep *The Secret*, then I will endeavor to explain why it is crucial to reveal *The Secret*.

Walls of secrecy are built around the victim due to several reasons. Some of these are threats of harm to themselves or others, threats of separation, or rewards which have been offered and given. The victim may feel enjoyment in the activity, either in sexual stimulation, or in feelings of importance; often this is the only affectionate physical intimacy experienced by the victim. *The Secret* may be kept due to *toxic shame*, an expression coined by John Bradshaw: "Toxic shame results from the unexpected exposure of vulnerable aspects of a child's self. The early shaming events happen in a context where the child has no ability to choose."

As *toxic shame* develops, the child stops trusting his own eyes, judgment, feelings, and desires. Dr. Suzanne M. Sgori, author of *Handbook of Clinical Intervention in Child Sexual Abuse,* refers to this stage of sexual abuse as the *secrecy phase,* one of the many phases of child sexual abuse. Most children understand the necessity of keeping *The Secret* to mean that the experience was too horrible to tell about, which in turn tells them that they, too, are horrible. *The Courage to Heal* furthers that assessment in that, "What the child learns then is not to trust; it's not safe to reveal the truth, and so they learn shame, secrecy and silence" (93-97).

I was told that if I revealed *The Secret* to my mother, she would die. I said I *needed* to tell her. The threat was reinforced with, "Do you want to see your mother in a coffin?" That possibility scared me enough to keep quiet for thirty-five years. My sister was told that if she revealed *The Secret* she would be sent to reform school for being horribly bad. That threat kept her silent for thirty-seven years.

Keeping *The Secret* leads to all kinds of problems for the victim such as addictions to drugs and alcohol. Depression and feelings of total isolation are two of many emotions that become problematic. I had to deal with prescription drug addiction and I still battle an eating disorder.

Telling *The Secret* brings about a transformation. It is the gateway to a road of pain and tears that leads to happiness, pride, self-esteem, and a certain contentment. Surviving *The Secret* tells that in the quest for survivorhood, relief will come when the abused (victim) looks for glimpses of meaning in his or her suffering (Vredevelt 158), and *The Courage to Heal* reveals several reasons for the transformation (Bass 93-97). Revealing makes it possible to start moving through the shame and isolation that has been felt, while making it possible to move through the denial and, finally to acknowledge the truth about one's child abuse. It is not until *The Secret* is revealed that a person can get help.

The truth helps one to get in touch with feeling in that once *The Secret* is revealed, the walls of resistance to emotions are lowered allowing feelings, long since denied, to rise to the surface. Most of the time this is a painful process, but only by going through the process can one become a survivor, rather than a victim. The abused person is able to look inward, into his or her experiences, through the eyes of a supportive person (perhaps a therapist, a good friend, created persona), thereby getting validation as compared to being seen through the eyes of the perpetrator where shame is acquired. In telling *The Secret*, the victim can make room in relationships for the kind of intimacy that can only come from honesty. It is through this honesty that one recognizes s/he is living now but dealing with the abuse of the past. The victim joins a courageous population of men and women no longer willing to suffer in silence, while becoming role models for other survivors of abuse. Eventually we feel proud and strong. Last, and perhaps most important, we may help end child abuse by breaking the silence in which it thrives making those around us in our communities aware that child abuse exists and what signs to look for in other children.

For me, telling *The Secret* made it possible to say, "See? I wasn't crazy. There were valid reasons for acting the way I did." Telling *The Secret* made it possible to finally inhale fresh air fully, instead of in short gasps. I felt as if I had just laid down a ton of weight—a weight that consisted of shame, gult, dirtiness and self-blame. I also felt very, very vulnerable, but refreshingly so. I realized how tired I was of feeling toxic emotions and only by telling *The Secret* and becoming vulnerable could I take the first step in ridding myself of those emotions. I also felt very scared. All of the *what ifs* came into play. *What if* no one believed me? *What if* what I remembered wasn't exactly as it happened? *What ifs* do not matter—telling *The Secret* matters. It is only by "confronting the truth of our childhood that we can free ourselves from destructive and self-destructive patterns of behavior" (Miller 38).

I once gave a speech in a college class in which I had chosen child abuse as a topic. After the class, a young lady came to me, her eyes brimming with tears. She said with great emotion, "I've never told anyone but I was molested for a long time." Her decision to finally reveal *The Secret* started her on her path of becoming an emotionally healthier person. This disclosure validated my decision to make myself vulnerable in a classroom situation by presenting a speech on this topic, and revealing an emotionally private part of myself.

Another time I was having a study group in my home and the subject of rape became the topic of conversation. I disclosed that I had been raped and how understanding my husband was concerning my history. I looked across the table to see tears streaming down a young lady's face. I asked her when it had happened. She replied, "I've *never* told anyone that I was raped."

Alice Miller, in *Breaking Down the Wall of Silence*, stated, "It's not the traumas we suffer in childhood which make us emotionally ill, but the inability to express the trauma" (Ibid.). The relief, for lack of a stronger word, in the faces of the two women I referred to above, were stories in themselves. To finally reveal *The Secret* that had been crusing from within as well as from without, is so unbelievably freeing. To finally utter the words, "This happened to me," is to start the healing process. Telling is transformative. It leads from a life of guilt and shame to one that is based on self-love and honesty.

It is essential to tell *The Secret* in order to start the nurturing process of the inner child, the once abandoned and betrayed child who lives in the soul of every abuse victim. This neglected child wants to be free of *The Secret*, for in getting rid of *It* the child becomes free of the speechlessness, isolation, and loneliness s/he has endured. In return, for telling *The Secret*, the inner child has a gift that only s/he can give: "It is the gift of truth . . . Ultimately it is the gift of security which our rediscovered integrity will give us" (Ibid.).

Often when *The Secret* is revealed it is not believed. The problem lies with the person hearing *The Secret*, not with the victim. It is extremely painful to tell *The Secret* and not be believed. It is necessary to choose someone as confidante who will believe *The Secret* and be attentive to the victim's needs. If *The Secret* falls on unbelieving ears, it is crucial to select someone else as a confidante.

Even though I have lived through this, it is still difficult to write without getting upset. I have been haunted by the words that were used to threaten me, and I resent what was taken away from me—the sense of my own power. It makes me angry that anyone would do that to a child, because if that child keeps *The Secret*, s/he joins the many *walking wounded* who are trying to make sense of their lives. I have seen the anguish on the faces of adult survivors still denying that anything happened, when down deep they know it did, but are afraid to tell—afraid to reveal the almighty *secret*. It just infuriates me, and I know where that anger comes from—my own experiences.

It would be wonderful to sit in a circle with all the abused children in the world and tell them that it is all right to tell *The Secret*. While doing library research for this essay, I was glad to find educational books for children (in the children's section) such as, *Sometimes It's Ok to Tell Secrets* by Amy C. Bahr, and *My Body Is Private* by Walwoord Girand. It excites me that abuse has become—although not as fast as any of us would like—a bad, five-letter word, that needs to be exposed for what it is.

I wish there was more education in the school system. It is alright to teach children to say "no" to drugs, but it is not alright to teach them to say "no" to save themselves. To me that does not make sense at all. Children need to be educated. If someone had told me, as a child, that it was alright to tell *The Secret*, I would have been spared so many years of anguish. The sad thing is that no one talked about those things then.

Well, it is time we talk about them and try to save children from the emotional devastation.

These are my core feelings. They come from much pain and anger, and are laced with love for the children who are being abused. I want to help young women and men by being the one who tells them it is okay to tell *The Secret*. My goal is to build trusting relationships so that these people know that I will treat their secrets kindly. This is what I want to do. There is something within me—pushing me. Helping others to get through their pain, in part, validates mine. Something in my head says there must have been a reason *The Secret* happened to me, and if I don't turn the experience into as positive an experience as I am able, then the entire trauma could destroy me. I will not let that happen because I have taken back my power, and I intend to use it by helping others reclaim theirs.

Telling *The Secret* is the first step to healing the emotional pain caused by the abuse. It is also the first step in reclaiming one's sense of power and reestablishing healthy boundaries in life. When I initially wrote my essay for inclusion in this book, I was aksed who the perpetrator of my abuse was. At the time I was unable to answer due to inappropriate timing of the question. "There simply were too many people at the gathering Laura (co-author) and I found ourselves. I shall elaborate here. Several men violated me, one from the time I was four until I was twelve. Another man took up where he left off, for about a year and a half—until my family moved to California. The next abuser was a teacher. It is as if a perpetrator has a kind of radar, leading to vulnerable girls—and girls are especially vulnerable once they have been molested because it becomes a way of life. My freedom came in breaking the pattern—in exposing *The Secret*.

Telling *The Secret* can lead to happiness and tranquility, and it must be divulged. The life you save could be your own.

WORKS CITED
In *The Secret*

Bass, Ellen and Laura Davis. *The Courage to Heal.* New York: Harper & Row, 1988: 93-97.

Bradshaw, John. *Healing The Shame That Binds You.* Deerfield, Florida: Health Communications, Inc., 1988.

Hyde, Margaret O. *Cry Softly! The Story of Child Abuse.* Philadelphia, PA, 1986: 7.

Miller, Alice. *Breaking Down the Wall of Silence.* New York: Penguin Books, Ltd., 1991: 3, 38.

Sgori, Suzanne M., M.D. *Handbook of Clinical Intervention In Child Abuse.* Lexington, MA: Lexington Books, 1982.

Vredevelt, Pamela and Kathryn Rodriquez. *Surviving The Secret.* Old Tappan, NJ: Fleming H. Revell Company, 1987: 158.

Author's note: Since this essay was written, Ms. White has received her Bachelor's and Master's Degree from Fullerton State University, California, and completed her internship in family counseling. She currently has her own practice, specializing in cases of child abuse. One's past does not have to deter one's future, proving once again that negatives can be turned into positives for the benefit of others.

ANGIE'S SHAME

A Study In Futility

L.L. Ames

There are some individuals who suffer child abuse, tell *The Secret*, but their sadness falls on deaf ears. Some tell *The Secret* and are told to keep quiet because of religious shame or family disgrace. Finally, there are others who disclose the abuse perpetrated on them only to be thought of as crazy or overly imaginative. The individual in this story, Angie, experienced every rebuff mentioned. She has suffered for over twenty years with self-inflicted guilt and shame. She finally gave up trying to get help and today she presents herself to the world as a very despondent and physically ill woman. Her story reinforces the necessity of seeking help and not giving up until that help is found. Sadly, this story represents too many people who fear the repercussions of exposure, and whose lives are forever affected in a negative manner—physically, emotionally and spiritually.

Angie had been brought up in a deeply religious home. Her mother prayed daily in the living room, kneeling before an alter and a lighted candle. A picture of Jesus adorned the wall above the alter and the combined effect was that of a shrine held in great reverence. Angie, a shy child, was very obedient, adaptable and somewhat compliant with all adults. She thought of herself as very happy, eager to please others, and always willing to learn new things. She was a good student in school and was well adjusted and energetic, a typical ten-year-old. She was also religious, as was expected by her God-fearing parents. To Angie, they possessed one major failing in her regard. Their old fashioned beliefs did not allow her to be as socially active as would have been normal and healthy for personal growth, and she was not well informed in the ways of the world or in the sexual complexities of her own development.

In the early 1960s when Angie was ten, she and her family moved to Bakersfield, California. The family's world consisted of traditional values, work, school for the children, and the church. Most of their waking hours revolved around the church and the move provided them with a new vista in which to expend their religious energies.

Angie's young age was not a deterrent at the church, and she was given a Sunday school class to teach. She was a devoted member of her faith and believed that her church was a great benefit to her. The Pastor was a friendly man and people enjoyed his sermons and his outgoing nature. He was a frequent visitor to Angie's home, willingly sharing his time with the family. Their move seemed a positive one.

For Angie it was a short-lived sense of peace before a series of events took place that altered her life dramatically, caused her permanent emotional scars, and created a deep sense of personal shame.

Just prior to Angie's 12th birthday, the Pastor began coming to the house while her parents were at work. During his first surprise visit, he physically shoved Angie against the wall, then against the sofa as she pushed herself away from the wall and tried to walk by him. Her brother was also home that first time, and the Pastor asked the two children if they would like some ice cream. When they excitedly responded, the Pastor told them they would have to play a game first. He told the boy to lie on the floor in the kitchen on one side of the table, Angie on the opposite side of the table. The Pastor then lay down upon Angie, assuring her it was part of the game he was playing. He instructed her to place her legs around him as he touched her body. Nothing else occurred that day. Angie experienced a strange, new pleasure from the encounter, yet felt an unbearable awareness of shame—as if an evil spirit had entered her soul.

Angie cannot remember any sexual incidents after that initial visit from the Pastor, but she felt violated and dishonored. (Her extremely self-effacing personality and the shame she still voices, however, lead one to believe that she was sexually abused by the Pastor many times and has completely blocked the experiences in defense of her emotional salvation.) Because of her strong religious beliefs, she could not bring herself to believe that becoming a young lady meant sexual maturity and that some of her physical response to the encounter was normal. She blamed herself for being evil. Somehow she was at fault for the Pastor's fall from grace.

As the days passed, Angie's school performance suffered. She became depressed and withdrawn. She wondered why no one noticed that she had changed, and that caused her depression to become more pronounced. It was as if no one could see what was happening, that she must be truly bad or people would ask why she was so unhappy. She finally quit high school because she couldn't concentrate and her depression deepened.

When she was 18, Angie joined Job Corps, a group whose purpose it was to help young people finish their high school education while training them for future work. She was sent to Maine for fulfillment of the Corps's goal, finding an air of serenity because she was away from the person who had caused her deep depression and dislike of herself.

As the two-year program neared its end, Angie dreaded her return to the place where the Pastor still lived and led his church. Out of desperation, she disclosed to a staff member the fears she felt. A job in New York was established so that she did not have to go home.

Angie doesn't remember her New York experience. She cannot recall how she went back and forth to work, what her job was like, if she enjoyed it or what she did during her free time. She does remember that her depression was taking over her life. She lived inside her depression. It was her companion, her nemesis, and a constant reminder that she was obsessed with demons because of her past shame.

Her return to California was a blurred, dreamlike experience. She does remember that she was suicidal most of the time, depressed all of the time, and was beginning to seriously doubt her sanity. She was eventually institutionalized where mistreatment, rather than psychological therapy, was the norm. Shock therapy resulted in permanent neurological damage to the left side of her face. She was placed on medication for the depression and when she tried to tell someone—anyone at that point—what had happened in her youth, she was simply medicated with more antidepressant drugs. It is not surprising that Angie spent most of her adult years in and out of mental hospitals. It was in such a place that she met her first *friend*.

Angie's fear of trusting another person was so profound that it was difficult to establish lasting relationships with either men or women. During her late 20s, however, she met a woman close to her own age who befriended her. Angie believed that a break-through in her emotional state was near because she had finally found a friend with whom she could communicate and who would understand her and relieve her loneliness. To an objective observer, it may have been apparent that Angie's new found friend was a user of people, with her own aberrant needs. To Angie, who still did not understand the whims and/or evil of people, the friend represented liberation from her sense of isolation and human interaction. It was only a matter of time until the reality of her new companion's demands forced Angie into a vortex of shame so catastrophic to her libido that her desire for marriage, a healthy sexual relationship with a mate, and a family of her own, died and to this day has never resurrected. "Without treatment, the experience (sexual abuse) can blight a child's life" ("Hidden Victims" 18).

Angie and her female friend decided that leaving Bakersfield would be beneficial. They moved to Tucson, Arizona, found good jobs, and began a fresh, seemingly unencumbered, life. As roommates, they were able to afford their own apartment, buy their own furniture, and be independent of their families. For the first time since the shame of her Pastor's behavior, Angie felt worthy and happy. The peril of this new relationship and the move was the fact that both young women still suffered major, unresolved mental health problems.

One dark, sweltering morning, just before dawn, Angie was awakened from a deep sleep. She thought she was still dreaming as she felt her roommate's hands roaming over her semi-naked body. She lay perfectly still, hoping she would awaken before she became physically ill with revulsion. "What's happening?" she heard herself scream, but no sound could be heard in the hot, early morning air. "My demons have returned." Again, no noise penetrated the silence of the bedroom, but the terror of her words permeated her soul. She silently denounced her God and with total compliance she allowed her roommate to begin a sexual relationship she thought was the work of the devil. She had been taught that homosexuality was a sin and that those who allowed it and lived it were evil with no hope of repentance. She believed that she should die for her sins. She wanted to die.

Angie felt trapped. She hated herself and the roommate who had professed to be her friend. She couldn't work, she didn't get dressed during the day, and she rarely ate. Her physical health worsened along with her mental stability. Voices were telling her to run away, but she had been so compliant all her life that running seemed an impossible solution. She continued in what she refers to as her sick relationship for almost two months, then could tolerate no more. She left one day while her roommate was at work.

To Angie the only salvation was death; her only thought was death. Upon returning to Bakersfield she once again sought help, only to be given more pills. Pills were okay, she thought, because they hid the truth from her consciousness and if she did decide to take her own life, the pills would facilitate the process.

Years have passed since Angie returned from Arizona. She has never received the therapy she so desperately sought. She is totally, emotionally disabled at this time, receiving Social Security disability benefits. She suffers a myriad of health problems: colitis; headaches; severe menstrual discomfort and other female-related disorders; back and feet pain; and a constant feeling of ill health. "A lot of research indicates that long-term severe affective states, like depression, influence the immune system" (Kemeny 197).

Whenever Angie seeks help through county health services, she is invariably given more anti depressants and literally shoved out the therapist's door. After such encounters with the *system*, she fears it will continue to reject her innermost needs.

Angie may never be emotionally stable. Unlike Leah in "*The Secret*," and Jean in *Saturday's child*, Angie no longer has the physical strength to pursue emotional wellness. She is currently living in an extended care facility and has been adjudicated a Public Guardian. She has given up all hope of ever cleansing her own soul of its pain and self-inflicted guilt.

As Leah White stated in the previous essay, "Telling the secret can lead to happiness and tranquility but it must be divulged—to someone who believes you. The life you save could be your own."

The message is clear: Don't give up. Please.

PART I

AN EMOTIONALLY DECAPITATING HELL

BEGINNING

The Painful Road To Sanity

"You must get inside your mind," Susan, my therapist, tells me as we begin the long road of the healing process. "You will be on a journey into your past. Now, try to focus on a house. Inside that house will be your sanity. Outside that house will be the pathway you will take to reach your destination."

No, I think to myself. There are too many hurdles. I cannot get down the pathway. Can't this therapist see that it is strewn with hate and abuse and sadness?

"As you encounter each deterrent in the path, we will stop and explore what it is and why it prevents you from going on."

Oh, God, must I do this? Why have you been so far away from me that you have never seen my tears fall? Am I bad?

"Some of those obstructions can and will be dissected, opened to display that which hurts and offends. Then we will go on."

What will I be giving up if I travel that rough road that has secured me to this place in my mind of madness and emotional pain? Wouldn't it be easier to leave things as they are?

"When we have destroyed or negated all the garbage on the path, you will reach the house and find security and sanity within. But, first, you must imagine that house."

3

I try to imagine a *safe* house, but what I see in my mind's eye is the long, painful pathway that leads to the first house where I lived—the house where the anger began. I can see myself—the skinny little baby nicknamed Cookie. Odd memories return and I wonder why my parents call me *Cookie*. I feel neither sweet nor desired. It must be a bizarre misnomer, just as my life has been referred to as *normal*. I seem to be angry, even at the age of two, as I suck in my breath, and remain that way until my face turns blue. My parents stick my head under the water, saying to each other that it will stop the tantrum and the anger. Which, of course, it does not.

As my therapist continues to encourage me into a more secure place in my imagination, she assures me softly, "The inner child in you still controls your adulthood. One day you and she will merge into an entirely different entity, becoming unified in your safe house."

I can see and feel the non-child in the child's body and even though Susan's words may be true, I fight an impulse to scream. I tell myself to hang on tenaciously to the child I was not allowed to be. I silently admit to God that I don't really want to be an adult yet. I beg Him to please let me grow up. I am confused.

I look at Susan and nod as if agreement with all she has said though I secretly think otherwise. Skillfully she guides me into returning for a second session. Before I realize what is happening, I agree that it is time for my journey to emotional wellness to begin.

As you, the reader, travel with me into my past, please bear in mind that the first two sections are written as if they happened to someone other than me—an objective observer. Many times I open *windows* in the narrative—highlighted by *italics*—in the present tense. These occur as my therapy progressed and my past became more related to my present—as my inner child, *Cookie*, and the older me, Jean, resolved our subconscious conflict. It was a long journey, but well worth the time.

> "Of all the agonies of life, that which is most poignant and harrowing—that which for the time annihilates reason and leaves our whole organization one lacerated, mangled heart—is the conviction that we have been deceived where we place all the trust of love."
>
> —Bulwer

THE JOURNEY BEGINS

It was May 23, 19_ _. Within a small, depressed house located on the corner of a desolate street in a hot, dry, California town, a story of depravity of a most hideous kind was beginning to unfold.

At The Tower, the name attached to a local hospital by some as the Bastian against outsiders, a few blocks away, a baby girl was born into the family who lived in that house. Their detachment from reality would provide the child with a destiny full of hatred, sexual abuse, and isolation. Ironically, the baby was born on her father's birthday and thus, named after the man who would take her as his child concubine, physically and emotionally, by the time she was three years of age.

I know the memories are distorted, hazy. Joan (my therapist after Susan moved away) thinks the pain and sexual abuse began much earlier because of a picture in my mind where I see the naked, lower half of a man standing over me. The man has a full erection, but the picture fades before I can isolate the incident or the identity of the person who belongs to the body—though I continue to try.

The baby's name, Jimmy Jean, was set aside like a dirty diaper and her Mommy and Daddy nicknamed her "Cookie." A reason for the nickname was never volunteered, and Cookie never felt a compulsion to ask why. Perhaps the reasons were as distorted as the family's values and their reality.

Cookie was small and thin, hardly a wisp of a child, with a worrisome demeanor for one so young. She cried much of the time in the early months of her life. As she neared her first birthday, the crying stopped. Though the desire to cry remained, the child was becoming too afraid of her parents. They impressed upon her that she would be punished if she cried, usually by a slap in the face. "Suck it in," Daddy would say. "Don't you cry." The baby was so angry, so afraid, and so frail. Such a sad little baby, and she seemed to hold the weight of her entire world on her tiny shoulders.

Sometime during her second year, the whispering began, perceived as her parents' way of keeping secrets. "Something is wrong with the baby's leg," she heard Mommy whisper to Daddy one day. "It needs to be looked after by a doctor."

"Why?" was the whispered retort. "We don't want people knowing our business."

"Because," Mommy replied softly, "it looks serious enough to cause a real problem if we don't go to the doctor. Then people would really question us if she died or something."

Not only did Mommy win this time, it was good that she did. The child had a boil just inside her left thigh that had reached an advanced stage of infection. The only option for healing was surgery, which was performed at the local hospital, the place of her birth.

In the hospital Cookie remembers waking up to see two doctors standing over her. They were so big, and she was so little. She was frightened because of their masks and the railings which surrounded the bed on which she was confined. Their menace may have been because their physical appearance was hidden behind their masks—*hidden* like all the secrets in her home. Though Cookie could not verbally express this unreasonable fear, she experienced it nonetheless. As a result, Cookie endured her pain in silence since her parents seemed to ignore it anyway. She was learning to hide feelings, just as her parents hid their actions from the outside world, and whispered around the children so they could not hear.

When I was an adult Mother told me she had a similar scar as the one created by the boil, in the same place on her own leg. For a brief moment I felt a kinship to this woman who professed to be my mother, a connection to the biological and emotional being who, at times, I questioned God whether she was even my true parent.

By the time Cookie was three, her actions belied her years. She seemed much older, as if part of her childhood was already missing. Her father had even schooled her on the use of the telephone is case of an emergency. It was this new knowledge that aided her when her mother's long, black hair was caught in the washing machine ringer.

"Cookie, call your grandmother," Mommy instructed.

She did as she was told, climbed up on a stool in order to reach the phone, and after three tries, Grandmother answered.

"Grandma, Mommy's hair is stuck in the machine," her little voice pleaded.

"Your uncle and I will be right there," she replied, not asking any questions, just acting on the fear she sensed in the young child's voice.

Cookie could see her mother, bent over, with her head up close to the ringers. Her mother didn't cry. Cookie stood back and watched as Grandmother and Uncle took the ringers apart to pull out Mother's hair. Still, her mother didn't cry, nor did she cry when she cut her beautiful, dark hair—an angry response to the accident, perhaps as a defense against the situation repeating itself and a reason for cutting the beautiful hair her abusive husband admired. At 19 years of age, Mother was teaching the young Cookie that one doesn't cry, no matter what or who may cause pain.

"I don't cry anymore," Mother told me recently. "I don't fight anymore, with your father, and I don't cry anymore." Her tone seemed to scream at me, "I don't cry anymore because I don't remember how."

So many lessons were being taught—so many feelings being repressed. Cookie was learning much faster and deeper than her parents would ever suspect, or even care to know. She knew that to cry, no matter what caused the tears, brought a strong, brutal slap on her face. Deep within her, she knew that the punishment was more severe than necessary. She listened to what was happening in her small world, and her confusion, sadness, and depression grew.

The *secrets* began. "Don't leave bruises where someone might see," Mother told Daddy. "Someone might turn you in."

I was shocked when I remembered those words. For so many years I tried to keep Mother separate from the atrocities being done to me by my father. Once I realized that she was a part of the shame and degradation being foisted on me, I found myself wanting to withdraw again, to a comfortable place. Mothers do not allow such things to happen to their daughters. "Mothers who tolerate such behavior (incest) or are too passive to do anything about it, are failing their children badly" (Ames 219).

It was also during this time—when I was three—that I became consciously aware of the sexual abuse. One particularly difficult session with my therapist caused this realization to finally penetrate my resistance to explore many horrible memories. Although reluctant, I was better able to look back at the littered pathway of my life. The road was very dark, however, and I was terrified of the dark. There was no one with me, to hold me and tell me I was okay. Nobody traveled that road with me. It was as if I was outside myself as I watched my father in his bedroom, in the dark, under the covers, and I was beside him. He struggled to rape me anally, and when this did not work, he drew me to him under the covers and began fondling me. Even this memory of an incident that certainly was not isolated makes me sick to my stomach.

The fear which resided within Cookie's small mind was with her constantly, causing physical as well as emotional problems. "Mommy, my chest is moving," she complained day after day. Finally, what appeared to be heart palpitations frightened Mother into taking the child to a physician.

"Your daughter is high-strung and nervous," the doctor diagnosed. "It is a common condition in some children and will probably resolve by itself as she gets older."

Mother did not tell the doctor that Cookie was terribly afraid of people, that she wouldn't talk to anyone, or that she tried to hide whenever people outside her family were present. And all the while, no one questioned why she was withdrawn.

As the sexual abuse became more frequent, Cookie's father told her, "If you tell anybody what Daddy is doing in the dark, you will be taken away and never see your family again." She reasoned that no matter how bad the abuse was, it was worse not to have anyone at all.

The sexual abuse continued for what would seem forever to this sad, lonely child. "Incest occurs in families where there is a great deal of emotional isolation, secrecy, neediness, stress, and lack of respect" (Forward 142).

I can see the child—me—walk down that dark road. This time, other people are going with me. I am not alone. Susan and Joan, my therapists, help me around the awful rocks and litter in the road. Slowly I began to believe that I could eradicate the debris and have a normal life, but not before I came to terms with the part each member of my family played. It is imperative that we who have been victimized as children understand we were not to blame; the entire family is dysfunctional because of the abuse. My story, then, becomes the story of many.

> "A goodly apple rotten at the heart;
> O, what a goodly outside falsehood Hath!"

> -Shakespeare

BEHIND THE FAÇADE

Living in a family such as mine was terrifying, of course. I never realized that how I viewed my life and how the outside world viewed it were very different. One method of hiding the horror, as well as controlling my siblings and me, was through religion. My parents created such a fear of God's retribution that we didn't dare rebel. Our seemingly perfect behavior in public would provide a picture to outsiders that we were good people who were perfectly normal. Therapy helped me put this controlling device into perspective so that I could better understand the process of keeping secrets. I continue to be amazed that my parents not only used God as a weapon, but that they managed it so adeptly.

In my mind, I can hear Mother's voice, always controlling—each thing she did to be substantiated by scripture from the Bible. She does this even now, yesterday underlining a passage in my Bible: Job 38: 1-2, "Then the Lord answered Job out of the whirlwind, and said, 'Who is this that darkeneth counsel by words without knowledge?'" At first, I thought Mother's intrusion into my Bible offensive, and I am certain she meant it that way—that she was trying to tell me how wrong I was to place my secrets in the trust of counsel outside the church, counsel without knowledge. Then I realized that her interpretation was totally different from mine. It was a revelation to me. The scripture passage was simply asking who dare "bad mouth" (darkeneth) counsel without knowing what the hell was going on. She had done it again, as she did when I was a child, but this time, I didn't see through the child's eyes. She could no longer control me with her Biblical words, taken out of context to suit her own actions and justify those actions which almost devastated the child, Cookie.

The year was 19—. Though the war years were past, the country was just beginning to bring itself under financial and emotional control. People were taking stock of their lives and progressing in what was to become an era of economic gain. To regain a sense of normalcy after the trauma of war, people became, what is referred to today, *socially* correct. Cookie's family, far from normal, did follow this protocol and became, to their small world, the *perfect family.*

Whatever their true identity, it was hidden by one very simple, public exposure. They were a Christian, *Bible*-toting unit. Cookie's parents knew either by former teachings, or in fear of *being found out*, that *secrets* were much better hidden if the outside world saw Christian parents with well-behaved children dressed in their Sunday best, marching behind Mother and Father in timely fashion each Sunday morning. The children were afraid to do otherwise.

Father offered up his daughter as sacrifice to prove to other church members that he was in control. If any one of the children misbehaved during a church service, Father would march him or her outside and proceed to whip the child without mercy. Yes, he showed the world that he was a good parent through his brutality, and he was sure the world believed it.

On several occasions I was told, "You have such a nice father." I was sickened by the memories and amazed that Father and Mother hid the abuse and sadness extremely well. We all looked so normal. "As with physical abusers, most incest families look normal to the rest of the world" (Forward 143).

The children were afraid that God would smite them dead if they misbehaved. One of Mother's favorite scriptures was: Ephesians 6:13, "Children obey your parents in the Lord: for this is right. Honour thy father and mother; that it may be well with thee, and thou mayest live long on the earth."

She neglected to add Ephesians 6:4, "And, ye fathers provoke not your children to wrath; but bring them up in the nurture and admonition of the Lord." When Cookie and her siblings brought this latter passage to Mother's attention, she denied that it existed or that it did not apply, wanting only to force her children into compliance with fear. And Cookie was afraid.

Mother was locked into her own fear of Dad, and she possessed an abusive skill which may have surpassed Dad's. Her beatings of the children were vicious and full of anger, but her ability to emotionally freeze them out of existence was devastating beyond their comprehension. Cookie didn't know how her brothers and sister felt, but she was convinced that she was not worthy of Mother's love for she was neither pretty nor smart.

Mother and Father, the pastor, the Sunday school teacher—they all said the same thing: Colossians 3:20, "Children, obey your parents: for this is well-pleasing unto the Lord." These people never gave *reasons*, only words from a book to be feared, written about a personage to be feared.

As an adult I learned the rest of the scripture from Colossians 3:20-21: "Fathers provoke not your children to anger lest they be discouraged." Why hadn't my parents read that passage? I could only guess that it did not fit into their scheme to make us children totally submissive to their combined sickness

Yet, Cookie, more than any other member of the family, believed what she was told and clung to the one person whom she felt cared—God. It was not a God of her imagination, but a God she learned about through her church, the *Bible*, and her mother's selected scriptures. She feared and loved this God, this protector, this "*God as our Father.*" Even when the other family members did not attend church, for whatever reasons, Cookie did. She associated the church with love and protection. And when her own curiosity questioned how God could allow her, a mere child who went to church and obeyed so diligently, to continue to be brutalized, she felt that somehow she must be *bad*. So she helped perpetuate the ruse. She went to church to avoid separation from family (her conception of death). She believed that if she did not obey she would die.

The abuse was hidden beneath an outer structure of sanity and Christianity.

Deformity of the heart I call
the worst deformity of all;
for what is form, or what is
face, but the soul's index,
or its case?

-Colton

THE PLAYERS

As Cookie Knew Them

By the time Cookie was six and a half, all the players in the family were cast. They were unwavering in their characterizations, hiding and abusing and fearing. The parts were somehow interspersed and intertwined; the players themselves served in each role, at different times, depending on their need to do so.

Mother, though not the most physically brutal or abusive of the parents, played the major role in Cookie's young life—for obvious reasons. The word *Mother* conjured a picture of nurturing, loving and bonding. In Cookie's world, in feelings that she could not yet put to words, she felt that *Mother* meant love and a protective demeanor. She saw Mother, however, as being unattainable, a person who never cried even though this woman-child—for she was only 16 years old when Cookie was born—was always sad. She rarely smiled, her features taut, strained and without emotion. Only her eyes belied her manner for they were full of sorrow.

Her eyes look sad to me now. Bitterness has been added to my perception of this woman who I now realize never came remotely close to the story-book description I had of Mother.

Mother had dark brown hair and was very thin. Even her physical appearance did not meet the story-book standards. There was no kindness in her eyes, no *bounce* to her step. She was plain and old, though only a teenager who had had no childhood.

Cookie was aware that Mother did not fight the system, either the one in which she found herself, or the outside world where she mingled only briefly on Sunday mornings. She wore dresses most of the time as dictated by the church, clothes that did not exaggerate her feminine sexuality. Cookie never noticed Mother using her arms or hands when talking, either to family members or others, like most people did. Her body was held in check, as were her emotions except when she was uncontrollably angry. At those times she would scream wildly, arms flailing.

In my mind, I see a strange woman who represented my mother. She was a very angry person, standing with her hands on her hips, screaming at me, the veins and capillaries in her face turning a deep purple. Angry words spewed into the air—so many words that eventually found themselves falling on my agonized soul. Otherwise, she spoke very little. Now she no longer measures words that constantly decry my association with the counselor, nor when she belittles me to my daughter, telling her the only reason I am taking a college creative writing class is so I can tell the whole world lies about the family—to expose them as being monsters and not the loving parents Mother insists they were.

Father, on the other hand, was loud and frightening when Cookie was a child. He was the Boss of the family, personifying a brute who had absolute control and power. All the children were afraid of this man who stood six feet tall and appeared as a giant in comparison to their small sizes. His blue eyes flashed meanness, yet to Cookie he had a sad face. Even then she tried to find something good about her father. Sadness seemed good because it meant that he was human and was suffering. This may or may not have been true since he never talked about his background with any emotion.

Father was a large man, in height as well as girth, weighing close to 220 pounds. When he spoke or commanded, his entire body became involved. His hands moved erratically, attacking the air around him as if it, too, was his enemy.

He now stoops, his six-foot frame lessened by age and a beaten demeanor. His once dark, straight hair is no more, having turned gray and thin. His formerly loud, powerful voice has turned sour, no longer intimidating. He appears smaller and as I continue into counseling, his threat to my emotional well-being becomes less and less.

Cookie, the first born into this disruptive, cruel atmosphere, was very thin. She looked emaciated and once the school nurse thought she was ill. Even her light brown hair was thin and wispy, falling straight upon bony shoulders. Her small nose rounded out the picture of sparse frame and fragility. She was teased constantly about her size and accused by her sister of being so ugly no one would ever want her. By the time Cookie was a teenager, she was convinced the family was right; she felt unwanted, helpless and afraid. As was their shared birthday, ironically, Cookie resembled her father.

A few years ago I saw a picture of myself as a child. I was not ugly. When I confronted Mother with this new knowledge she replied, "I know." She did not offer an explanation as to why she and the others tried so hard to make me believe that I was unattractive. I may suspect the true reason for this unkindness, but I probably will never know just what motivated them to do as they did.

Cookie was a very rigid child. She possessed so many secrets that holding herself erect made her feel impenetrable from the outside world. Her small elfin face displayed the sadness and pain that she worked very hard to hide.

When I saw baby pictures of myself, the sadness in that infant face reached out beyond the time dimension, pleading with me to go backward and fix the past. What atrocities had already befallen this new creature with the old face? I shudder as I write, trying to remember. I'm not sure that even now with my therapist's help, I can confront what must have occurred.

Cookie used no body language other than her face when she spoke—which was very little. She rarely spoke to adults and was so reserved and fearful, she had no friends. She was a lonely child, locked in fear so horrendous she forced memories in the farthest reaches of her immature intellect.

Twelve months after Cookie's birth, Mother's second child was born. The year was 19—. The new baby was stocky, with blue eyes and brown hair, resembling neither Father nor Mother. From the moment he arrived into the dysfunctional family, in Cookie's perspective he was a difficult child. He seemed to fight everything from giving up the security of his bottle to potty training. He rejected all the rules set forth in the house and was constantly in trouble either at home, at school, or in society, holding back nothing. "If his mother is cold, unpredictable, and hostile, he learns before the age of a year to mistrust all people to a degree. His own mistrust will in turn arouse unfriendliness in others" (Spock 87).

According to some child abuse theorists, if a child tells his/her Mother that s/he is being mistreated by his father, s/he is beaten by the abusive man who claims not only biological kinship, but made in the image of what God expects of fathers. The child's honesty and needs are ignored by Mother, the person he relies upon to protect him.

Mother told me on the day Dad decided to kill himself that there had been other children he had abused. Now she will not talk about any of what took place during my youth. She has closed herself entirely, and many times denies having ever discussed the matter. She is in a constant state of denial. This frustrates me, though I know deep down that I cannot alter her behavior.

Cookie thought her brother to be very brave and she held him in secret admiration. He defied the angry father and learned to ignore the subservient mother. Whatever fears he may have felt, he kept them well hidden.

It is now clear to me that he, too, was a secretive person, and his aggressive behavior may have been his method of keeping the family secrets. This is a revelation to me for I thought he was my only sibling who had the capability to defend himself from both the abuse and the neglect. It is odd that when I admired him, I also felt his pain, and how sad I feel at this moment that we cannot be brother and sister in the true Biblical sense—loving and emotionally close.

In 19—, another brother was born. The older boy was now three and Cookie was four. (Cookie was being sexually molested repeatedly. She may have wondered if she would not be at Father's mercy so much of the time since there were now other children.) The new baby was a placid child, never getting into trouble, easy to care for from Mother's view. "He is a good baby, with such sweet behavior," Mother commented repeatedly. Cookie was convinced by this constant reminder that the baby was a better child than she, and she wondered what was wrong with her that caused Mother so much bother after she had been born.

Mother continues to impress upon me that her youngest son was a good baby and I was not. In the back of my mind I know that he was not a better person, but the pain of Mother's words still cuts me emotionally.

The youngest boy was not only an outwardly good child, he was like Mother in many ways which endeared him to her in what little capacity she actually had to love and nurture. He enjoyed music and art, and so did Mother. He did not display emotion verbally when he was hurt or suffering, neither did Mother. Psychologically they were kindred spirits in many ways.

Because of the insidious behavior of the humans involved, there were flaws in Mother's nurturing. The boy stuttered. Many times Mother would join Father in his unmerciful teasing of the young boy's affliction. Cookie felt so sad and ashamed when her parents would entice the toddler to recite: "Hubba, hubba, ding, ding. You've got legs and everything." Father or Mother would say it first, then insist the little boy repeat what they said. Sometimes when other members of Father's family lived in the same household, they would be willing participants in the mean game, laughing when the child would be in tears, perhaps his sense of self-worth withering even more. Whatever nurturing Mother had given, she took away during those moments when she made fun of her son's speech affliction. What mixed messages this sad little boy was receiving.

When the boy entered kindergarten, he began wetting his pants—further confirmation of internal unhappiness. Presumably, it would have been apparent to normal parents that this child was deeply disturbed or physically ill, both of which could cause an already potty-trained child to present with the symptom of *wetting himself*. But, of course, this made no difference in the lives of these parents who were bent on destruction, in whatever mental illness they both resided.

Even though Cookie's brother may have been suffering, he did well in school—a child's attempt to gain approval of his parents. He may have felt that by being a *good boy* he would be left alone.

I can see my younger brother and sister standing with Mother, talking to each other. I felt as if they didn't care, as if I wasn't even there—like a non-person. Although I don't remember specifically being jealous, I think this one incident which stands out in my mind may have been the beginning of this emotion. I know that I felt anger with my sister, Mother, and Father, but I never said anything to anyone. I simply became more withdrawn.

The youngest baby's birth almost caused Mother's death, yet she was nurtured more because of it rather than less—a much more normal response.

How odd, that sitting here, right now talking with my friend, we thought Mother's close call with death may have been a religious experience for her—that somehow it absolved her of some of her sins for the Bible talks about how a woman will get married and give birth to children and sacrifice her life for them. Maybe, because Mother almost died giving birth to her fourth child, she was doing what the Bible required and expected of her.

Mother's new-found ability to nurture did not, however, provide the youngest girl protection from the physical and emotional abuse. Cookie overheard Mother talking about an incident when her sister was crying about Father and said so.

Father's response to the accusation was, "It must be the youngster's imagination." That was the end of the discussion.

Cookie's sister was a chubby, cute baby who resembled Mother and received much attention from both parents. The sickness of the father didn't stop with this child, and the result was she, like the other children, became as secretive as they. Cookie was never able to determine what was going on with her sister, both girls being equally rigid, and Cookie sensed that her sister did not like her, though she did not know why.

I still feel a sense of loss in this area because I have never understood. One day I talked to my sister as we walked to Mother's, but the subject wasn't broached. The opportunity has not presented itself because now we do not speak to one another at all. This was brought home again the other day when my daughter, Kay, and I were walking back from the grocery store and encountered my sister walking toward the college. She spoke to my daughter, "Kay, I won two thousand dollars in the "Rubber Ducky" contest! I bought the ticket for the contest because the man had been nice to you when you were younger." Not once did my sister look in my direction or acknowledge that I existed. This was plainly an affront and I do not know if she and I can ever be more than strangers to one another. From my earliest memory of my sister, she was always trying to get me in trouble whenever the opportunity presented itself, or when she could manufacture trouble and convince my parents that I was the one to blame.

Cookie watched one day as her sister rubbed her arms until they became red and bruised-looking. "Why are you doing that?" Cookie asked.

Without turning to look at her sister, the youngster ran to Mother, screaming and crying, "Look what Cookie did!"

Cookie was not asked if this was the truth, but instead, received a beating for being mean to her younger sibling. Her sister had learned to transfer her pain to Cookie. She had no way of knowing that Cookie was being sexually abused, and she *needed* someone else to suffer along with her and she chose her sister.

The setting was complete, the roles had been cast, and the play began. It continues to run more than forty years later.

> "Lull'd in the countless chambers of the brain
> our thoughts are link'd by many a hidden chain;
> Awake but one, and lo, what myriads rise!
> Each Stamps its image as the other flies."

-Pope

SUCK IN THE ANGER,
HIDE THE MEMORIES

During one emotionally exhausting session with my therapist I turned to her and said, "I can see myself, with my head under the tap water, my father screaming to my mother that the cold water would stop my tantrum. I can feel myself gasping for breath—then the blueness of my face beginning to recede." So many memories pour forth, and still I cannot pinpoint the very moment in time that the sexual abuse began. I was two years old when I used the breath-stopping method of dealing with my anger. Of that I am certain. Was that when it began? I cannot remember so long ago. Or is it that I do not want to remember the pain, the shame, and the degradation?

At the beginning of 19—, life in the household was changing drastically. Cookie was eight months old. Her mother was 16 and pregnant with her second child. A mere youngster herself, Mother was finding herself tied down and out of emotional control. It was easy to allow Father to rule the family and take the pressure away from this sixteen year old wife and mother.

I have wondered many times if Mother had to get married. It would explain so many things: why she was only 15 when she married; why she didn't like me; why she allowed father to have the upper hand; why she always seemed so sad and desperate, so unable to cope. I asked Mother once if she had had to get married, but she changed the subject. One of my friends suggested that she may have been raped by my father, and because of the era in which she was raised, she may have been forced by societal rules to marry regardless of the circumstance of brutality. Yes. It makes a sick, sad kind of sense.

At eight months Cookie was still a somewhat normal baby. She was eager and curious and Mother often complained that she simply could not keep up with her antics. Cookie was constantly climbing out of the playpen—the one place Mother could keep the baby confined and out of her way. When Mother tried to change her diaper, Cookie scooted away, and Mother angrily pulled her back into position. Mother's own pregnant condition, emotional subservience to Father, and her youth didn't allow for patience or nurturing for her child.

By evening each day, Mother was worn out and emotionally drained. She wanted the baby out of her sight and mind. Cookie, as with many children of eight months, was active well past bedtime. In order to insure that Cookie remained in her crib, Mother began pinning her under the blankets at night, forcing the child into submission—taking away her natural need for movement and seeking comfort during her sleeping hours. Messages were being given to this tiny person. So many messages. Not only were her emotions to be confined, but her very existence of being a living, breathing, active human were being denied through physical control. She could not verbally express the deep frustration she must have felt, for she did not have the power of speech. By the time she was talking, she had already learned not to express her feelings—that to do so would get her into trouble with Father, whose wrath would manifest itself as a beating with a belt on Cookie's thin, frail body.

Had the sexual attacks begun then? The more I work with Joan and the Group, bits and pieces of memory start falling into place, but can a memory be brought from the depths of babyhood—prior to the skill of speech? I don't know, but I have this recurring impression of being in a crib and outside the crib a naked man stands with a full erection. Did he do that to me then? I am beginning to suffocate, as I always do when memories of this kind come forward.

Cookie's awareness of the constant bickering between Mother and Father began to form with substance by the time she was two. Her parents never seemed happy and she wondered if she were at fault for their unhappiness.

I felt for a long time that if I hadn't been born, my parents would have been happier. Even now after all the counseling sessions, I wonder how different their lives would have been without me. My intellectual self tells me that they are and were very sick people. My emotional self still tells me from time to time that had I been different, they would have been different and thus, happier—loving me in the way I wanted and desperately needed. According to my therapist, most children of abuse are confused as to whether they are the victim or the cause of the abuse.

The boil episode comes to my mind whenever I fall into the "What if" trap. I was two years old at the time. I consciously became aware of my surroundings and the actions of the people within my small world. Because of what I know now, I most likely attributed the pain and subsequent surgery to God's way of letting me know I was not worthy of my parents' love. Why else would I be such a bother? Vaguely I recall Mother explaining away the infection as a black boil. Maybe that was her way of letting outsiders know that the infected boil was not her fault—today, she still repeats, "Nothing is my fault." Obviously sufficient care had not been given to the infected area, and it had been allowed to fester, becoming contaminated to the point of needing surgery. Father did not believe in taking children to the doctor, and it was most likely his unwillingness that prevented me from getting adequate medical care as soon as it was needed. Did my father beat me when I cried because of the pain created by the infection? Is that why Mother finally took me to a doctor, to keep me quiet and therefore, keep my father's anger in check? He didn't like to hear us kids cry, and would spank us when we did. He screamed some stupidity such as, "If you don't stop crying, I'll rip your arm

off and beat you with it. That'll give you a real reason to cry!"
Yes, we learned over and over again, to keep quiet. Illness was
something else again, and I am sure that as with all children, we
had no control when the pain became severe. Mother will not say.
I think that somewhere, in the darkness of her soul, she suffers
from a great deal of gluilt and continues to block the memories,
distorting them as she so often accuses me of doing.

Cookie, though very young and constantly belittled for
her presumed stupidity, was nonetheless, a very bright child.
She learned quickly and even responded to the emergency of
her mother's hair being caught in the washing machine ringer
with confidence and maturity, getting help for her mother's
distress. Cookie was also very aware of what her father was
doing to her; she knew that it was not right.

Two years ago my counselor, Susan Amon, told me that the
type of sexual abuse perpetrated on me when I was three is called
sodomy. To this day, the emotional and physical pain haunts me
whenever the subject is discussed. The shame I feel is overwhelming,
and I want to curl up in a fetal position and hide.

I can see a pathway that leads to the first old house, and a
lot of pain is strewn on that pathway. I wish that nice things had
happened then, but I cannot remember any. All the dark pictures
keep appearing.

Cookie's first verbal memory of Father being a part of her
existence was when he made his living by driving a cement
truck. Mother was confined to the house and the care of her
young children. Throughout her married life, she never held a
job outside the home.

She once told me she never had a job because she was unskilled.
I don't recall ever thinking she was unable to work at something
other than as a housewife and mother. I do remember feeling great
embarrassment and shame that my father was illiterate.

The house in which the family lived during Cookie's early
memory of the sexual abuse was old and run down. It had a
brick-look siding made of asphalt that Father eventually applied
a new coat of paint to in order to make it look cleaner. There

was no grass surrounding the house, although there were some trees that Father had planted. The first room upon entering the house was a large, square living room. An old brown couch and matching chair, along with a special chair for Father, were the sparse furnishings to a drab, depressing room. There were two bedrooms, one for the parents and one for the children. The house did not have a kitchen; a building behind the main house served this purpose. A stove, refrigerator, sink and table provided the sad family a place for meals where constant tension and fights occurred, either between the parents, the children, or both. The room was as dark and foreboding as the family that utilized its facilities. The bathroom was in the main house near the parents' bedroom. There was no carpeting on the floors for warmth; instead they were covered with a dull, brick red and black linoleum. Periodically Mother would Purex everything, almost in a frenzy to sanitize that which was unsanitary in her opinion—or possibly some compulsion to try to ignore the drabness and cleanse her own soul of its guilt.

The children were not given blankets for cold, wintry nights. In turn, they could each be heard crying, "I'm so cold." If they shivered and complained enough of the cold, Father would cover them with coats. Father and Mother, however, had blankets.

It was obvious to Cookie that as children they were not worthy, or maybe Father derived great pleasure in subjecting the children to the elements for his facial expression when he covered them with coats was one of pure contempt and a sick kind of joy. He seemed to have a never-ending bag of hateful tricks to play on his brood, for he certainly did not consider them people.

We were not given blankets until I was a teenager, and only then because Grandma had made them for us—at no cost to my father.

It was in that house that Cookie was often sent to the bathroom to wash Father. She cringed inside when she had to wash his private parts.

"I don't want to do this," she would think in her childish way, hoping that her internal voice could be heard. "Why can't Mommy?"

Her pleas were to no avail for even if they could be heard, they would receive no response—no rescue from the inevitable. Father's demands were met and her emotional and physical resistance went unheeded.

When Father was hurting her she would try to think of anything other than what was happening to her body. She could send her mind off somewhere else, a place where nothing could be seen or felt—a dark place. Sometimes she experienced the physical pain, yet she was able to feel separate from it. Holding her breath made the pain more bearable.

I was talking to my therapist one day, trying to explain to her just what my father had done to my body, trying to put names to the body parts being invaded and how they were invaded. Suddenly, she raised her voice and asked what I was doing to my own body at that very moment. Subconsciously, as I began to unlock the memories, I sat in the therapist's office and held my breath—just as I had done as a child. Even at 46 I was still trying to keep the pain from becoming unbearable. I wondered how my mother would feel if she knew that I still used this method of hiding the past, the pain, and the horror.

I hated that house and what my father had done. It was there that he would take me into the bedroom when my mother went to church. I will not—cannot?—remember how the sexual abuse took form. It is still too difficult to cope with the fact that my biological father used my body for his perverse pleasure, as if I was nothing more than a toy. I do recall my father pulling down my panties in front of others and he and my mother would laugh, never caring how mortified I was. To complete their cruel behavior, they would say, "Cookie, you are split from ear to ear."

I could not understand why my mother allowed this. Did she ever stop to think of what it was doing to me? Was she again trying to placate my father by joining in his cruel teasing, perhaps taking the focus from herself and placing it on me? Am I still trying to explain away her behavior as being a survival tactic, still not facing the fact that this woman was and is mean?

By the time Cookie was four years old, she had two brothers, the older boy was three, the younger boy was one, and Mother was twenty. Three children and an abusive husband were taking their toll. Mother was subservient, broken-spirited, and physically old beyond her years. Her emotional state was still that of the child who had never been allowed to evolve naturally into anything else. Adulthood was forced and, therefore, inadequate. She lacked the years of emotional and physical growth which come with the normal process of being young, carefree, and unafraid.

Mother and Father were screaming most of the time by then, either at each other or the children. Cookie was very frightened by the turmoil and hid far away from the noise and anger. She cried a lot and found herself hoping that someone would come along and stop them.

Did I ever wish them dead? Perhaps I have blocked this from my mind because of the religious teaching of my parents and the church. I wonder if thoughts of death went through my mind as a child.

My friend has asked this of me many times, "Did you ever pray that your father would die? I know that I did, with the determination that I would not feel guilt if my dad should drop dead. I truly believe that many children have such thoughts where abusive parents are involved. Surely you must have wanted him dead."

I wish that I could remember. I think it would help eliminate some of the pain and guilt that I continue to feel as I travel along the pathway I need to think of as my road to sanity.

Unreasonable treatment and demands were made on the three children. "You must show the world outside this house that we are a normal family! You must not cry! What we do is for your own good! God wants you to obey your parents or He will punish you!"

Cookie watched as her brother responded with aggressive and uncontrollable, inappropriate behavior, while her other brother was placid and uncomplaining. Cookie was afraid. None of them knew how to predict the bad moments, or what caused them to be bad.

There were times when Father hid candy, then took it from its cache and he and Mother would eat it in front of the children with malicious satisfaction. Cookie and the young boys, who could not even put thoughts into words, were not certain whether this was a method of control or sadistic pleasure. The enticement for the children to seek out the candy on their own was obvious. "I wonder where that candy could be?" the parents would prompt. "Ummmm. Candy is so good. I just don't know where that candy is." Then they would both laugh.

How were the children to know about the mind games of the parents? Cookie, always a curious and somewhat gullible child, responded to the parents' questions by searching for and finding the candy. One day, as she was eating her treasured find, she was caught in the act by her parents. Mother held her down as Father beat her repeatedly with a shoe. "Naughty girl! Stealing Mommy and Daddy's candy without permission!"

Why? Why had it taken two people to give one little girl a beating? Had they been waiting for me to find the candy and thus, give them justification to administer their sick punishment? Of course they had. To this day, and if I have another 30 years of counseling, I don't think I will ever understand how parents can do such horrible emotional and physical damage to their children. And yet, at that young age, I still sought their approval and love regardless of their attitude and treatment of me.

By age four, Cookie tried very hard to be a nice person so that her parents would like her. She was quiet and for the most part, stayed out of Mother's and Father's way. She knew that her parents expected her to be a good girl and the church taught her to mind her mother and father. It was the Godly thing to do without question. This was impressed upon her many times with scriptures from the Bible.

My friend and I looked up a scripture that fit Father's aberrant behavior—in his mind—and why it was inflicted on us as a family: Timothy 3:4, "One that ruleth well his own house, having his children in subjection with all gravity." This was not a scripture quoted to us by Mother, and I am surprised that it was not, for it would have further justified their cruel punishments.

Normal young children might be wiggly at the dinner table, and picky about the food they ate, but Cookie ate everything on her plate and sat as still as possible. She did not want to be noticed. If she didn't follow the rules, no matter how small the infraction, Father would spank her or knock her down.

How well I remember the episodes around the dinner table and my compliance with my father's rules—and what I thought were God's rules. It no longer puzzles me that all of us kids grew up with eating disorders. One time, when my youngest brother was four, he wouldn't eat his stew. My father slapped him off his chair, onto the floor. To this very day, he will not eat stew. I cannot say I blame him. I, however, still find it very difficult to leave anything on my plate, whether I am full or not. Old habits and fear die a slow and painful death.

> Childhood is a period of our lives when time is
> unmeasured, life is easy and disappointments are
> few and far between. Or is it?
>
> —Rokelle Lerner

INSIDE OUT

Outside In

The stage was set by the time Cookie began school; she feared entering into the outside world. To break away from home, no matter how awful it was, was more frightening than the abuse she experienced in the hidden recesses of her father's bedroom, or the bathroom, or wherever he chose to molest her. Indeed, she was enmeshed in a horrible situation, but what if she broke away and accidentally told the secrets of the family? Cookie became more reclusive than ever. "Incest may be frightening, but the thought of being responsible for the destruction of the family is even worse. Family loyalty is an incredibly powerful force in most children's lives, no matter how corrupt that family may be" (Forward 147).

In 19—Cookie began kindergarten. She had already been well-schooled in the baser side of life. Emotional detachment relieved her of some of her pain. Going to public school meant she had to deal with outsiders and a new world which she was certain was going to be as bad as the inside world in which she lived. She was not looking forward to entering this new, horrible place with new and horrible people. She could expect nothing good because she knew nothing good. There was no joy or excitement to be found in this frail little girl at the prospect of going to school and being with children her age. She would never be able to learn the social amenities because she made sure that, emotionally, she would never be allowed into their lives. They in turn, would never be allowed into hers.

From the first day of school, Cookie was terribly unhappy. She was afraid of criticism from anyone and tried desperately to go unnoticed. When some of the school children learned her name was Jimmie Jean they laughed at her for having a boy's name. "What are you? A boy or a girl?" She didn't have the assertive behavior necessary to either explain the reason behind her name, or to defend herself from the cruelty of the other children.

The hiding process, having been so deeply entrenched in her psyche, began to take on excessive proportions. It was the only way to protect herself from those inside and outside the family. She was so very alone

Janet Worlets states: "I stay connected to my mother out of guilt, what feels like love. If I let go I'll be orphaned. She doesn't meet my needs, so I feel empty inside. If I let others fill me up, I'll cut myself off from her and I'll be an orphan, so I have to be empty." This very much applied to Cookie when she began school. She feared the loss of her dysfunctional family, particularly her mother, more than anything in the world, so she remained empty, alone and lonely.

Cookie's new teacher thought the child odd and made fun of the dark, dark, pictures the little girl drew during art time.

"What kind of pictures are those? What a silly child! Can't you do any better than that?" Harsh laughter would follow, and the teacher's unkind remarks made it evident she thought Cookie abnormal and strange, not necessarily emotionally ill.

When her mother learned of the dark pictures, she also criticized Cookie. "You are making the family look bad with those awful pictures. Are you totally stupid?"

The child was reaching out through her art, trying to tell whoever was available that she was hurting. No one paid attention, either because they didn't know how to reach back, or because they gave the child little credence as being a real person with feelings and deep emotional pain.

I think Mother may have begun to wonder whether or not someone might notice what was wrong with me, and she was afraid of the family secrets being exposed. Now that I look back, I can certainly understand the fear that motivated and directed my mother's very existence. Her way of making sure that teachers or anyone outside the family didn't notice me and my psychological baggage was to criticize me publicly, as if in agreement with those who saw me as different. As a child, being different from other kids is one of the most detrimental emotional burdens to bear. The loneliness cannot be described except to another who has experienced the same feelings. I find it difficult to express this kind of loneliness even to the Group or to my friends, though most of them have probably felt the same at some time in their own lives.

To Cookie, her four year old brother, was becoming more and more aggressive. He was, to her, brave because he was at war with the world. He fought the system; he fought with the neighborhood children. He was unable to get along with the children or the teacher in his Sunday school class.

I remember the mothers in the neighborhood coming to our front door, "You must do something about that son of yours. He is terrorizing the neighborhood."

To further Mother's distress, the Sunday school teacher verified what the neighbor ladies were saying. "Your son is totally disruptive in class. We cannot tolerate such behavior and you must do something to put an end to it or he will not be allowed to attend Sunday school."

Even though I was only five, I remember that my brother was good at throwing rocks, and that one day Mother went down the street to find out what new problem my brother had created. Mother whipped him and as soon as my father came home from work, my brother was spanked again with either a switch from a tree or Father's belt. If Mother didn't tell my father, someone in the neighborhood would, and then Mother would be punished. I felt very sad for my little brother when he was punished twice, as we all were whenever we did something our parents considered bad. The physical punishment hurt, but the emotional abuse was far more damaging.

"The Devil will get you too, after we are finished with you," both parents yelled. And we feared God and His punishment even more than that of our parents.

My brother, however, was the exception. He continued his aggressive behavior. A few years after I started kindergarten, he tried to hang our younger brother, who was four, and then later shot him in the face with a BB gun. I saw it as it happened and am still awed today by what I considered his actions when we were children: brave!

Cookie was in kindergarten when her youngest brother was two. He was so quiet, which seemed to be a totally abnormal behavior pattern for a young boy. He never gave Mother any problems and never bothered anyone else. He never explored his world, never cried, and never disobeyed Father. To Cookie it was almost as if he did not exist.

Mother continues to inform me: "What a good baby your little brother was and what a blessing he was being born after your other brother and you. Both of you were so bad and into everything."

How is it possible that Mother did not realize her second son had learned a different method of survival, and that he was just as emotionally injured as we? When did she stop seeing what was happening by establishing her own survival tactics? Oh, how I wish Mother would come to counseling with me so that 1 could learn the answers to so many of my questions. ". . . the mothers with the heaviest emotional baggage may be those who were themselves sexually abused as children"("Hidden Victims" 18).

Cookie thought that going to school made her important in the eyes of her parents, and she tried to please them, hoping for their approval. Mother, on the other hand, thought that preparing Cookie for school was a bother and complained incessantly about Cookie's unruly, straight hair. Mother was none too gentle during the hair combing sessions, repeatedly expressing her impatience, "Cookie, your hair is hopeless! I don't know why I bother." The little girl often wondered if it was the hair that was hopeless, or if it was she who was hopeless. If she was hopeless, what could she do to make it not so?

Mother also reminded Cookie that she looked like her aunt. "Maybe it's the Indian in you," Mother would say. Cookie knew that Mother hated this aunt and to associate her with her aunt must mean that Mother hated her also. How was she to know? How could she possibly respond to this kind of emotional abuse? She couldn't. She could only immerse herself deeper into the black hole of emotional repression.

At age six, Cookie's fear of the world outside the family was firmly established. Fear of her inside world—the real world in which she physically lived—grew as well until she was so afraid of Father she dared not say or do anything when he was near. She never knew what would incite the uncontrollable part of his anger, nor what would encourage the sexual abuse.

Cookie could not predict whether she would be slapped in the face or beaten with a belt when she misbehaved. When beatings occurred Mother stood back and watched, so frightened she wouldn't interfere. One time Mother reacted to Father's brutality, trying to prevent him from beating Cookie. "Leave the girl alone. She's so skinny. You might hurt her."

"Shut up, R-," he shouted back at her, "or you will be next!"

I wanted her to interfere, anyway, damn it! She was my mother and I needed her protection. Though I heard her cry when she did not notice I was there, that did little to resolve my own pain. After that incident, however, Mother cried very little. Apparently she was so frightened of Father's wrath that she dared not disagree with him—just as I dared not. As a child and well into my adulthood, however, I never credited my mother with having the ability to feel and react as my brothers, sister and I did. We had no other recourse, it seems, to be anything but what we had been programmed to be—all of us, including my mother.

Cookie's oldest brother was in school by then, and he hid very little. His anger with his life at home manifested itself in almost every action. He fought on the school playground, he fought in the neighborhood, and he fought in church. He irritated his parents to the point of repeated beatings and screaming matches Cookie witnessed. Although he was only five, he definitely wanted to let the world know that he was mad as hell.

When Cookie's sister, the youngest, was born the attitude of the family changed. She was the baby. She was cute. She was good. And the youngest boy, the placid little boy, began to display his anger, directing it at the new child in the household.

The year Cookie was seven, the family moved to Lompoc, California. She had just begun the second grade at Jefferson School in Tuften when the move took place. It was 19—. Mother was 23, the brothers were six and four and the baby was a year old. Father was 27.

Not one member of the family was chronologically old, but Cookie felt old. She was responsible for most of the housework by age seven, yet was restricted in everything she wanted or tried to do. She found nothing to be happy about. Sometimes she wondered if people outside the family could tell that she really was just a child who wanted to act as such.

Four children and an abusive husband had placed Mother in a permanent state of subservience and unhappiness. She had no personal desires or goals. She probably had nothing to look forward to except more of the same. She appeared emotionally dead and much older than she was.

The house the family moved into in Lompoc was ugly looking to Cookie—a little red place without indoor plumbing. There was a gas heater instead of a wood stove. Everyone took baths in a round tub in the kitchen, from water which had been heated on the stove. The household amenities of the late 1900s were as foreign to Cookie and her siblings as they were to children of the late 1850s.

Early one morning Cookie's mother was standing beside the heater warming herself when her nightgown caught fire. She ran outside and rolled on the ground to extinguish the flames. Her desire for survival was strong, though her life had little meaning. Mother treated the fire incident as she did all others—without apparent emotions. That same heater also caused Cookie pain. As she was trying to light the heater one day, it blew outward at her. This event caused Cookie to fear fire and stoves for many, many years. Her parents did not react in any way, not with anger or concern—almost as if the non-person had done a non-thing.

There was no fence around the yard, which was surrounded by empty, grassy fields. Cookie wandered alone many times, looking at birds and bugs. Her tenderheartedness caused her to cry one day over a meadow-lark a little boy had shot with a BB gun. Unlike her usual non-assertive self, she told the boy he was mean and she didn't like him very much. This one incident laid the groundwork for Cookie's ability to treat her own children with more kindness than she was ever given by her own parents.

The school was an unusual place to Cookie. All the students wore uniforms; the girls wore gray skirts and white blouses. This made Cookie feel good because everyone looked alike and the other kids couldn't tell that she was from a poor family. Cookie's teacher was a sensitive lady who detected a deep sadness within the little girl. She tried to tell Mother that something was wrong with her daughter, but Mother did nothing.

In my later years, Mother talked about it, telling me that the teacher said I had a problem, but that she (Mother) couldn't imagine what was bothering me. I don't remember the incident. I don't even remember going to church in Lompoc, which I find odd because we attended church wherever we lived. I do not remember the sexual abuse, though I'm sure that it continued there, as it had previously been part of my existence. My ability to block out certain areas of my youth may be due to the fact that the abuse was so severe that to remember may be detrimental to my present sanity. I do not have any answers yet, and I know that in order to finish my journey through the emotional litter, I must confront the hidden memories.

Sometime during the last two months of her stay in Lompoc, Cookie's arm was almost severed. She was running through a field and fell into a barbed-wire fence creating a four-inch, U-shaped gash in the middle of her left arm. A neighbor drove her and Mother to the doctor, Cookie holding her arm folded in an up position to prevent excessive bleeding. The doctor put clamps on the cut. The burning pain she felt when he did this was almost unbearable. She had no one to nurture her, nor hold her close and dry her tears.

I can feel the physical pain as I sit here and write. The scars from the clamps are still with me—a constant reminder. Before the wound had completely healed, I was allowed to spend a few days with Grandmother A. She was appalled. Her doctor removed the clamps, but it was too late to prevent the horrible scarring. No one questioned why I had run into the barbed-wire in the first place. Three years later when my eyes were tested, we learned that my vision was so poor I couldn't have seen the fence. No one had noticed the fact that my sight was defective. I wondered then (and now) whether my parents didn't take the time to notice, or if they just didn't care. I really don't want an answer.

I do not remember any other incidents that took place in Lompoc. I cannot remember what my family looked like, for the most part. I do know that my sister was a year old and I played with her a lot because she was quiet and easy to care for. My youngest brother was four and small. My other brother was always fighting and crying. He was a stocky kid with curly brown hair.

When the family moved back to Tuften less than a year later, Cookie and her brother were taken out of school one month prior to the end of the semester. Both children failed the grade in which they had been enrolled.

That year was the beginning of many moves and by the time Cookie was seventeen, the family had moved 17 times. The move from Lompoc to Tuften brought them back to the same ugly house and Mother attended the same church. Cookie and her brother returned to the same school. The family returned to the same cycle of emotional, physical and sexual abuse as if they had never been away.

Yes, my memory of sexual abuse at the house in Lompoc is gone. I can only imagine that it was so horrible I have pushed it into my subconscious, being more than my present emotional state can cope with or accept. What happened in the house on T Street, when we returned to Tuften, is not forgotten.

Sometimes Cookie's father took her places with him. These were not typical outings for a father and daughter. Father treated Cookie more like a date than a daughter, walking along with her, holding either her arm or her hand. When he found a secluded place, he sexually molested her, in whatever method he chose, by means that Cookie hid even from her conscious thought. She never wanted to go with this man who was cruel and unrelenting in his perverse sexual needs. She wanted to go places with her mother, but her mother wouldn't let her. Instead, she gave unspoken permission to Father to do as he wished with this child. Mother seemed happy to get one of the kids out of her hair. Often Cookie found a secret place of her own to hide and cry, becoming more and more closed.

During the next year, Cookie's relationship with her sister began to deteriorate. She couldn't understand why the little girl didn't like her, but this may have been when Father was more abusive to Cookie. Cookie reasoned that her sister must have been more compliant than the other three children because she seemed to have a closer relationship with both parents.

In later years I realized Mother had actually caused this lack of bonding between my sister and me by always blaming me for making her cry or taking her side whenever we argued. I do not know why.

Cookie never imagined that life could become worse, but it did. In 19—the family moved to Washington State and Cookie's total plunge into an emotional inferno was achieved.

> "O life! thou art a galling load
> along a rough, weary road."
>
> —Burns

ISOLATION

In April of 19—, Father went to Washington to establish a job and find a house in which the family could live. He returned to California in May, just prior to Cookie's ninth birthday, and uprooted the family again.

Mother told me that she did not like moving so often but she felt she had no choice but to do as Father wished. She said that if she had it to do over again, she wouldn't allow so many moves. Of course, this statement was easy to make, but I feel that had she to do it over again, Mother couldn't do anything but what she had done before. Without being someone totally different, a person with a different set of values and inner strength, Mother could only do what she was programmed by her circumstances to do.

Father never considered the emotional upheaval caused by these moves. He just did what he chose to do and if anyone suffered, he was either not aware, or he simply did not care.

They were always moving. One reason may have been because no one was happy and a move might make it so. Maybe the next house or next town would offer up a salvation of sorts. It never did. Most likely the fear of someone finding out about the family secret was the true reason for its nomadic existence.

Father rented a U-Haul, loaded all their belongings and set forth to their new home in Washington. He had built a type of camper out of plywood on the back of his old blue truck, furnished it with a brown sofa where the children, except for the youngest child, sat for the long journey.

Cookie slept during most of the trip. Her brothers and she did not dare fuss with one another out of fear. Father would pull over to the side of the road when the children misbehaved, take his belt off and whip them, one at a time.

The trip was at least 20 hours long, but the family members didn't stop to eat, go to the bathroom, or to stretch their legs—only for gas. Mother usually prepared food ahead of time to take on trips because Father thought it was too expensive to buy food along the highway.

For Cookie, it was easier to sleep during moves so that she did not have to deal with any reality whatsoever.

My memory is vague about that trip. I'm not sure whether I slept so much to avoid confrontations, or to shut out all the emotional pain. I tend to believe it was the latter. I have learned that excessive sleep may be a sign of severe depression.

The first structure in which they lived in Washington could only be called that, raised as it was off the ground on what Cookie referred to as stilts. This being the case, dogs, cats and other animals could run freely underneath and with more than enough room for busy, active children to explore.

Although the house vaguely resembled a house from the outside, it was anything but a home. It bordered the woods and maybe people who had known contentment within the family unit could have made it a happy place. To Cookie's family it was merely a temporary stopping place where more abuse would take place, leaving permanent scars and creating more bitterness in the heart of Cookie's mother.

The house itself was unpainted and its gray color made it look dry and dusty—the way it smelled to Cookie. There was no beauty, not even in the imaginary minds of the children. There was no toilet, no bathtub, and no hot water except what could be heated on a wood stove.

Each of the children took a bath in the same water. Cookie did not like that at all. Fortunately, they only bathed once a week. There was no privacy and the sister sometimes bathed with Cookie. Dad, at those times, wasn't in the kitchen. The girls weren't used to taking a bath in a large, non-installed tub, and they hated it.

There were no screens on doors or windows. To allow fresh air in was to also invite in whatever creatures flew in that air. Some animals had already taken up permanent residence in the walls and ceilings within the house—mud daubers nesting in the ceiling, bats living in the walls.

One night Cookie awoke to find Dad swinging a broom, unsuccessfully, at the bats that had come out of the walls in search of food.

This square-shaped structure consisted of one huge room and one bedroom. The sisters slept in the living room. Clothing and whatever other materials could be found as blankets were kept in the corner. Mother and Father slept in the bedroom with real covers and a real bed.

I cannot picture where the boys slept. They may have been in with Mother and Dad, or they may have been in another bedroom. Odd, that in retrospect, so many events are missing from my life. When I try to remember, I become agitated. My road to wellness is still so littered with garbage. Will I ever reach that safe house? Some days, I am not so sure.

The large, main room had walls that were papered with old newspapers, turned yellow and dirty with age. A big, black, wood stove sat on the left side of the room, along with the sink where it was Cookie's responsibility to do the dishes each day. The outside toilet had dried-up. There were unpainted boards on the exterior and an offensive odor on the inside caused by the defecation of many people, but had never been cleansed with the necessary chemicals to prevent disease and pestilence.

I remember being so frightened when I had to go to the bathroom outside at night. I made sure to go before nightfall. My brother had a kidney or bladder problem at that time and was so scared to go to the outhouse at night that he wet the bed. Finally my parents provided him with a can next to the bed. Since we lived near the woods, my greatest fear of going to the outhouse was the bugs and animals that lurked in the darkness. I could relate to my brother's fear and subsequent wetting of the bed, but couldn't understand why Dad spanked him when he did so, since his bladder problem was most likely a major contributor to the nightly wetting.

Outside the house, poison oak grew wild and uncontrolled, curling up around an old tree stump in one part of the yard. The land surrounding the house was covered with high weeds and grass, a perfect haven for a multitude of insects and small animals such as turtles and snakes. Across the road a creek meandered, seemingly as aimless as the family who lived within the house. Poison oak hugged the creek's edges as if to dare anyone to venture into the cool water. Wild blackberries and stinging nettle plants had overtaken part of the land. It was a wild-looking place, full of dangers and unknowns, yet the children managed to find some pleasure in their complicated world.

There were a lot of animals and we found that under the house was a place to hide. I liked picking the wild berries—they were big and tasted wonderful. All of us kids were interested in the animals, the deer that came right down to the back door. At that time, the respite from the pain I endured was found outside of my familial world. Going to church also offered much needed relief from the isolation. I remember that we were getting checked by a doctor one day and the doctor looked inside my underpants. I never knew why, but my friend now suggest that maybe the doctor suspected I was being abused by the way I acted. When I told Mother and Dad about what the doctor had done, they became very upset. Had they feared discovery of their abusive behavior? If this is true, then they definitely knew that what they were doing was wrong.

It was at this first house in Washington that Cookie contracted the skin irritation caused by the poison oak leaves. She suffered the entire summer from the affliction, itching so terribly she didn't think she could tolerate another day of discomfort. The patches of poison covered her arms and chest and Cookie felt as bad on the outside of her body as she did within—pain was, after all, pain. Her mother finally agreed to seek medical help where a physician determined the poison was also in Cookie's blood. She needed a series of injections in order to get well. Cookie received no sympathy from the family during her ordeal, and the pain from the poison oak was nothing compared to the pain within her young mind.

I woke up a lot in the night, having to deal with the pain by myself. I don't remember Mother ever attending to me. I felt as if no one cared about me or what I was going through. Mother and I talked about this episode several years ago. Mother said, "I don't even know what poison oak looks like." Was she trying to absolve herself by declaring her ignorance? There does not seem to be much of a mystery.

During the few months the family resided in that particular house, the brothers and sisters continued their path of isolation and their emotional deterioration. However, the youngest brother, the most openly sensitive of the siblings, was still able to display his delicate feelings about nature and the wonders it beheld. One day in particular he caught a large bullfrog, tied a long string to its leg, and staked the string by the creek. When he returned some time later, the frog was no longer in sight and a snake was attached to the string. He became very angry because the snake had eaten his frog. His anger quickly turned to uncontrollable sorrow. Mother, in a rare display of kindness, tried to comfort her son but he resisted her ministering because he did not understand them. He had learned not to trust anyone, especially a mother who didn't protect him from the brutality of his father. Instead he may have learned to hide a new kind of emotional pain—that to love something as he did the frog meant he would eventually be hurt. It was better not to open oneself up again to such emotion.

When the family arrived in Washington, the youngest girl was three years of age and was dressed to look like a boy. She had developed scalp ringworm prior to the move and Mother was advised that the child's hair should be cut off in order to allow the medicine to heal the area quicker and with greater efficiency. The baby girl (the parental favorite according to the other children) would be disfigured in Mother's eyes and she could not bring herself to comply with the doctor's orders. People might ask questions as to what was wrong, why the little girl had no hair. Having ringworm had a stigma: a catching disease that was their fault and they feared it would give credence to their inadequacy as parents. They didn't want to explain to the outside world, continually hiding whatever they felt was necessary to hide.

Using a ruse to get out of Mother's sight, Grandma Adler took the youngster and did the necessary deed. Mother was horrified. Her little girl looked like a boy. Fearing people would question why the female child had no hair, Mother began dressing her like a boy to match the shortness of the hair. Another cruel lesson being learned by the children was to never draw attention to the family. Hide all its secrets. Push them back—back into the recesses of the mind.

Cookie's younger brother was a quiet child. The teasing he received from his parents regarding his stuttering made him unwilling to talk. He may even have been relieved that he was not allowed to speak more often. He may have dreaded those times when he was coerced into reciting, and the family laughed maliciously as he stuttered out the words. A sad prediction for his future life.

I see this brother as totally withdrawn as an adult, not having anything to do with the family most of the time. None of us really know what he is doing or how his life is going. He is a very closed-up man—as his childhood lessons from Mother and Dad taught us to be.

Mother and Father fought most of the time, and the children followed by example. The internal anger of each member of the family was being acted on to the greater detriment of the progressively dysfunctional group. The children began to see Mother cry much of the time, which was totally out of character since she was so good at keeping her emotions in control. They were never told the reason Mother was crying, but they were very aware that something dreadful was wrong with their lives.

I can visualize Mother on the bed, lying on her stomach, crying. I felt so afraid. I cannot remember if I was afraid of her, for her, or for myself. I do not even know if I felt responsible, and that was the greatest fear of all—not knowing how I fit in to all that was happening in my life and the life of the family as a whole. Many of us who have been victimized as children are confused about our place in the world. Counseling helps us to put our lives in perspective.

When in the company of people outside the family, Mother was noncommittal and reserved; she did not show tears, nor emotion of any kind. Father was very vocal whether with the family or not. He ruled everyone with the force of a madman. What he said had to be adhered to or physical punishment to one or more of the children was imminent. He did maintain some male friendships, but would brag about getting into fist fights with people from work. He was a violent and abusive man, inside and outside the family unit.

Today, Dad is a wasted man—old, stooped, very gray and defeated. He sits all day long, watching television, smoking cigars, and drinking Pepsi. He is through fighting. When we were children, Dad had a lot of male friends visit the house. Now, no one comes. He is truly all alone.

When the family lived in their first Washington house, Father took the children to work with him, a different child each day. When Cookie's turn came, she was filled with anxiety and fear, knowing what Father was going to do to her on the way. Cookie wished that the day was over, that it would soon be tomorrow.

Father pulled off the road, into a secluded part of the woods, before getting to his job as a logging truck driver. From that point until the end of the day, Cookie's memory of the incidents was totally obliterated, except that she knew Father had hurt her. She simply blocked out the horror of her father's abuse.

I still cannot focus on just what my father did to me. I know it was sexual, but as a child of nine, I do not know if he penetrated my vagina with himself or an object of some sort, as he had done before. I was angry deep within. I did not understand why this big man was hurting me. I went outside myself, looking in on something that had nothing to do with me. I could not have coped otherwise. I remember that I wished I could curl up in a ball and hide from the pain. Curled up in such a way to prevent the pain from coming in, no one could see in, and I felt as if I were invisible. Who could hurt me if they couldn't see me? It's odd, but when I was writing down this sequence of events in Washington, I began thinking of the Sword of Damocles, which was a test of the precarious balance between happiness and unhappiness. I feel as if I have had the sword of Damocles hanging over my head all of my life. In-depth counseling has yet to reveal what the extent of the sexual abuse was that took place during those days of my life. There are times when I believe we really don't need to uncover all our past memories, particularly the very bad ones.

One early summer morning at the "new" house, Cookie reluctantly got out of bed and pulled her coat up beneath her chin. She shivered with the feared expectation of her day. Would Daddy come take her for a ride today? Would she have to go to work with him? She struggled with these thoughts in her young mind—a mind that should have been filled with the joys of childhood. Cookie threw the coat away from her body, the only blanket allowed her for the cool nights.

Instinctively she knew that this morning she would have to go to work with Father. She lived close to the woods and as she watched the birds flying above her head, she wished she could be just like them and fly away from all the bad things that happened. On this particular day, she fantasized that she arose early and went into the woods with the birds where she could hide from him. As she climbed the tree, she could hear her father calling and calling. His voice echoed through the woods.

"Cookie! Cookie! Where are you?"

She was suddenly brought back to reality. Maybe if she stayed in the tree, Daddy would take someone else to work. She knew this would not be because her father kept the sexual abuse *fair*.

Father decided to move again in July, after only two months.

I never knew why, but my imagination runs away with me as I try to speculate and analyze why my parents' behavior was not normal, or at least what I considered to be normal in families. I believe my father moved every time he thought it would be discovered he was a child abuser. My imagination tells me that as crazy as he was, he must have known the law and he feared going to jail. It would ease my mind to know that he suffered from guilt for his actions, but I don't think that he did. I remember reading: "Intentional abuse indicates that the parents are emotionally disturbed and require psychiatric help" (Clayman 263).

The move had little effect on Cookie. She knew that trouble followed wherever they lived. A place was just a place. Nothing could make it a home. Another shack like the first greeted the family with a sense of forlorn and violent prophecy. It seemed to Cookie that such places had to be for families like hers. Again, it was isolated in the woods, far and away from people—another place to hide the abusive addiction of the father.

The house was built out of green wood. The smell of pine was pungent, itself abusive to the young children's senses. Sap ran out of the wood and down the walls in streams. All four children slept in the single-room attic—the boys in one bed, the girls in the other. There were no other objects to contradict the function of the room as being anything but a room with beds. It was an attic with no floor covering, no carpet. Cookie could see through the cracks in the ceiling down into the room where the dining table sat.

It was in this room that one of the boys knocked over his pee can, causing the urine to drip down upon that dining table. After that, he was forced outside to take care of his bathroom needs.

Cookie, from her vantage point in the attic, could witness Mother and Father at the table talking, Father with his coffee in hand. She found that by spying on her parents, she could learn things that weren't discussed in front of her and the other kids. She didn't know what she expected to hear, but she knew that she was doing something Mother and Dad wouldn't like. Perhaps that was the joy in doing it.

The house had no toilet, inside or out. Everyone tromped into the woods whenever necessary—no privacy, no pride, no civilization. It was frightening for Cookie to go into the woods at night. When she woke early in the morning and she had to use the bathroom, she laid in the dark and wished the feeling to urinate would go away. When finally she could no longer hold it, she would run into the woods, void, then run as fast as her thin legs would allow, back into the safety of the lighted house.

I suffered most of my life with bladder infection after bladder infection. Is it any wonder why? Seeing this in print for the first time, I realize that my physical problems had a basis of which I was not aware. Even in the case of illness, I somehow thought I was to blame. To this day, I beat myself emotionally whenever I am sick. What did I do wrong? Where did I fail to take care of myself properly? These thoughts and "persistent health problems seem to go together for many of us who have suffered the ongoing stress of abuse" (Kemeny 197).

Cookie began the fourth grade that September. The school building was a pleasant place, with several large oak trees and an unfenced play yard. Kindergarten through high school was held in the same building, which meant that the younger children were at the mercy of the older students. The bus also served all students, again providing a place for the bigger and stronger boys to pick on the smaller children. One boy, in particular, was the bully of the group, teasing Cookie and her brothers with a buzzer he carried in his hand. His teasing was unrelenting, and Cookie was intimidated and afraid. She had a strange feeling about this boy.

Cookie spent her recess and lunch period under one of the huge oak trees, playing with acorns—all alone. For her it was a safe place to play and the solitude allowed her the time to wonder about what was happening in her life.

I used to wonder why the people who should have cared about me never seemed to. An aunt told me, when I was an adult, that it was known that Dad treated me badly, but everyone was afraid of him and, therefore, allowed the abusive behavior to go untold to anyone who may have been able to remedy the mounting problems within the family framework. If someone had said to me, "I know that you are hurting and I love you," my life would have been more tolerable. I didn't know anyone who really cared about me. The sexual abuse would have gone on unchanged, but I would have had someone to hang on to. So I sat under the oak trees and wondered, as usual, what I had done.

Cookie wished she was back with her grandmother. Grandma A and Cookie played games and did things together—things Cookie should have been doing with her mother, such as sewing and drawing.

One day when Grandma was visiting she told Dad, "You are treating your children—my grandchildren—wrong."

Dad, red in the face from his fury, shouted at Grandma, "Shut your damn mouth! It's none of your business!"

Grandmother A, angered beyond words, quietly left. Fear kept her away, kept her from helping or getting help, although during those years child abuse was not talked about much. To even get the authorities to help was next to impossible, regardless of whether the adults were abusing their children, or the children were abusing their parents.

Cookie did have one friend and though they weren't as close as best friends, the little girl provided Cookie with one happy memory from her life in Washington. During their leisure times, the two girls delighted in riding a little brown pony. When the two rode at the same time, the pony lay down and refused to move. The girls were amused by the pony's antics and their laughter was a refreshing sound to Cookie. She had a brief taste of normalcy, and discovered that she liked it very much. A friend was new to her, something she had never had before.

During the school day, however, it seemed to Cookie that she didn't exist in anyone's eyes except her own. Even her new-found friend did not acknowledge that Cookie was alive. Cookie accepted the behavior from her friend because she expected it. She was used to emotional abuse from everyone as a well-trained, abused child learns to be. She was no longer curious why she was the brunt of such negative actions. She knew it was her fault and must be tolerated. In the back of her mind—in what was left of her sanity at that time—she heard a loud voice screaming, "Why?"

One night, shortly after school had begun, Mother and Father left Cookie home alone with the boys while they went shopping with their three-year-old daughter in tow. As soon as the parents had left the house, their landlord's 17 year-old son came to visit. He screamed at the boys to go outside to play. Frightened, the brothers did as they were told. When the teenager and Cookie were alone, he pushed her down onto a brown, wooden table. He climbed on top of her and began to unzip the front of his pants. Cookie, scared and desperate, began to scream hysterically. Her brothers ran back into the house, terrified themselves but wanting to see what was wrong with their sister. Cookie's attacker ran out of the door, but not before he yelled at her, "You keep your mouth shut or there will be hell to pay!" Silently, she agreed.

Cookie was sobbing out of control when her parents returned from town. For once, Mother bothered to ask what was wrong, but Cookie kept still for she knew if she said anything, there would be a big fight and there was enough of that already taking place in her life. She was afraid Dad would kill the boy, so violent was his nature. She did not tell anyone of that incident for thirty-five years.

The Monday after the attack, Cookie was afraid to get on the school bus. The boy who had attempted to molest her was the same bully who teased the younger children every day on the ride to school. He was standing by the bus when she arrived, smirking as if he had been waiting specifically for her. On the bus, Cookie kept her head down, hoping no one would notice that she was frightened or different because of the horrendous experience.

Cookie rode the bus with her attacker for the next three months, fearful every day. Her thoughts were only on the teenage boy, whether he would try again and be successful the second time. Her fear grew and her pain grew. Cookie had a new secret. To her there were two different types of secrets. One was not to tell anyone that Daddy was doing things to the private parts of her body—things that hurt her. Father told her over and over that she must never tell this secret and her fear was so great, she didn't.

The other kind of secret involved things she didn't tell Daddy, Mommy or anyone, secrets she knew would make them act awful. She couldn't tell Daddy the boy had tried to rape her. She couldn't tell Mommy that Daddy was making her do things that weren't right. Mommy and Daddy might blame her for these happenings, and she was afraid that if she told, there might be a fight. She couldn't bear the fighting.

Cookie's anger grew toward her parents because of all the secrets; sometimes she wished both parents dead.

At other times she fantasized that Mother would call her in from play and say that Daddy was dead. She tried to imagine how she would feel. Of course, guilt always followed.

"Do ye hear the children weeping, O my brothers ere the sorrow comes with years. They are weeping in the playtime of the others, in the country of the free."

From: SOMEWHERE A CHILD *IS CRYING*
—*Vincent J. Fontana*

BEYOND HELL

Thanksgiving Day, 19—, the family packed up their meager belongings to begin the trek back to the town from which they had come. It was a cold, gray day, full of foreboding for Cookie. How apt that the weather should match the depression within her own soul. What bits and pieces of sanity were left to the family was not known, but Cookie's young heart and mind knew not to expect the move to make life any better. In fact, she was certain it would not.

Father's blue truck was the same as it had been when they had arrived in Washington the previous May. The three older children were placed in the back of the homemade camper, and the baby was seated up front with Mother and Father.

The day before Thanksgiving, Father killed five skinny chickens. Cookie cleaned them and Mother fried them to be eaten on the long ride back to California. There was snow on the ground as they pulled out of the drive which led up to the shack in which parents and children had lived during their six-month stay. Silent, very personal, humiliation and shame were among their belongings, and were as tangible a reality as the sadness that etched the expressions on their faces.

As Father drove closer to the Washington/Oregon border, fog settled in, and the gloom of the day was complete. Hope for a better future was not a part of the wretched family, and happiness was just a word with vague meaning.

Hitched to the truck was the U-Haul trailer in which the family dog had been secured with a rope. Miles after the trip began, Father stopped to urinate. He decided to check the U-haul, for an unknown reason. The door to the trailer was open, and the rope on which the dog had been tied, was dangling over the back bumper. The dog had evidently fallen out somewhere along the road. Everyone was sad, and the children began to cry for their lost pet. Mother didn't cry.

A flicker of an image: Dad crying as we all stood by the side of the road, on an isolated stretch of highway. Did he cry? Never before had I seen him do so—only that day in 19—when the discovery of the missing dog caused us all to be upset. Did he cry? Did I wish him to cry and that is why I have this memory? Crying is such a normal response to sadness and I believe all of us who have survived abuse wish our families could be normal.

Father would not backtrack in order to find the dog, "It could be too far and I don't want to waste any more time." So the family continued as if nothing had deterred them.

Since the return to Tuften, California, was an unplanned, hurried affair, the family did not have a house awaiting their arrival. Grandma A agreed to let Mother and her family stay until such time a house could be found. Although Grandmother and Father were normally at each other's throats, the brief stay proved uneventful and calm. Within two weeks, Father had a job and the family was uprooted once again to their new home in Dusty Flats, ten miles east of Tuften.

Dusty Flats during the late 19—s was a tiny, isolated community surrounded by dry, brown hills. The surface area was covered with a fine silt which was distributed and redistributed each time the wind blew—almost a daily occurrence. There was very little greenery, and what did exist was on an individual house basis, nurtured by the tenants therein with care and piped water. It was an arid land with an average rainfall of just under four inches per year. It was a sparse land that held little outward beauty, except perhaps to the artist or naturalist who appreciated the beauty of desolation and sterility.

Cookie's emotional stability suffered when she saw yet another shack in which Father forced the family to live. The house, which may have had paint at one time, was in such a state of disrepair that the paint had been stripped by weather and age. It had two bedrooms, the biggest given to the children—the girls in one bed, the boys in another. The walls were papered with the news of times past. There was a living room, furnished with the family's ragged old chairs and a couch. The kitchen was as much a mess as the remainder of the rooms.

I have tried, so many times, to remember what that house looked like inside, but I cannot focus on anything except my depressed state during the year we lived in that horrible place.

At least the house in Dusty Flats finally provided the family with indoor plumbing, complete with a bathtub and toilet. For this, Cookie was grateful. She didn't have to fear trips to the bathroom, outside in the dark.

The exterior of the house was overrun with weeds, alongside the outer walls and throughout the yard area. The perimeter was encompassed by a broken-down, bare wood fence—a broken down family, once again, living in a broken down house, in an isolated stretch of humanity, continuing its broken down methods of control and intimidation. It was a sad, sad time. There was more and more violence. Father became angry, for whatever reasons or no reason, and grabbed the children, hitting their heads together. It is a mystery why none of them suffered broken bones or permanent head injuries. Mother lashed out at the children with any available object, it mattered not what damage could be wrought with her weapon of choice. Cookie often found herself the object of Mother's anger, with her head being battered against a wall. She was becoming more and more confused as she tried to understand or learn what she had done wrong—what caused Mother's behavior to be so violent against her.

I can only assume that Mother knew what Father was doing and rather than confront her own inaction in my defense, she directed her anger at me. I was devastated by the unfairness of Mother's actions, confused about the reasons, and concluded in my mind, that it was somehow my fault. I am still questioning what part I may have played in the violence of the drama which unfolded daily within the family. I know that when I let go of what I surmise is my own guilt, I will let go of the shame I felt so many years ago. Another obstacle in my road to peace will have been overcome. We, who have been abused, particularly by both parents, share a kinship of sorts, especially in regard to the guilt we feel.

The family continued to present to the outside world what it thought was normal behavior. By going to church, and using the church against the children, the parents assured themselves that the secrets would go undiscovered. They could validate themselves as productive members of their society. Luke 12:3 "Therefore whatsoever ye have (done/spoken) in darkness shall be heard in the light." Luke 8:17 "For nothing is secret that shall not be made manifest neither anything hid that shall not be known and come aboard."

Cookie was allowed to go to church only if Father deemed her worthy. He exercised his reward by checking every space of the house for which Cookie was responsible to clean, even looking under beds and behind furniture. If so much as a speck of dust lingered, Cookie was denied her Sunday school privilege.

In 19—, Mother presented me with what was left of Grandma A's diaries. In one of them I read a passage which said, "I feel so sorry for Cookie. Her father checks under the bed and if there is any dust, he won't let Cookie go to church." I knew then that I had been loved very much by my grandmother, even though she had little control over what had taken place because of her own fear. When I asked Mother why she didn't read her mother's diaries, she sneered, "I don't want to read them." This was the way my mother always dealt with reality—passed it to someone else to analyze so that she did not have to face it, and could criticize the analytical thought of anyone other than herself. Mother's reticence became clear to me one day when I read: ". . . often they (mothers) have denied their own abuse for so long that they can't accept what's happened to their children" ("Hidden Victims" 18).

It was while in Dusty Flats that Cookie began to question some of the things being taught in the church. She was nearing puberty, and her curiosity and concerns may have been triggered by the physiological changes going on within her body. She found herself asking God why He was allowing her life to be as it was. If He was truly a loving God, why didn't He love her? Where, she wondered, was her guardian angel? She saw that some people were protected, and others were not. What made people so different that some suffered and some were happy? Her conclusion was that since no one—not Mother, Father, nor God—loved her, she must be a really bad person.

I continue to question the validity of my worth. I do not look upon myself as a bad person, yet when I encounter rejection of any kind—reasonable or not—I tend to take the blame. I am so tired of being this way. I am so very tired of the shame and guilt and low self-esteem. My search for answers must not give in to such thoughts for they cause me to feel as if I am going backwards.

Uncle M, Mother's brother, died the year after the return to California, and Grandma A was depressed. It was tradition for the family to spend Christmas with her, but because of Uncle J's death, they were already together. The family battles were becoming more and more filled with anger and frustration. Holidays were no exception and Christmas, though a Holy day, was just a day of more of the same. With depression and the death of her son, Grandma spent much time at the house, including that particular Christmas, and was a constant thorn in Father's side. She openly disliked Father, and though afraid of his physical violence, very rarely held her tongue.

The family, as a whole, retained the status quo of their life as it had been in Washington. Father, however, began to attend church on a regular basis. He went up to the alter one day, professing to change and not do bad things anymore. Cookie felt such a sense of relief because she truly believed that he meant what he was saying in front of everyone—else why would he be so public with his words? Cookie was unable to express how she felt when she learned his words had absolutely no meaning, that he had lied. She found herself hating him more than ever, and questioning the truth of God at the same time. In her young mind, she could not understand a God who would allow such a man as her father to exist.

It was after Father's open lie to God and to the people of the church that Cookie began to have thoughts of suicide. Her depression was completely overriding everything she observed or in which she participated. "Suicide results from a person's reaction to a perceived overwhelming problem, such as social isolation . . ." (Clayman 953). Her problem was how to end her own life. An eleven year-old, not wise in the ways of the world, could not imagine a viable way to do the deed that would free her.

... with distorted values
the mother unknowingly destroyed,
took the mind of a child
and created a void . . .

—L.L. Ames

THE VOID

Most of the time Cookie felt like a person separate from her family of origin—emotionally, physically and intellectually. No one was a part of anyone else. Everything and everyone was disjointed and dysfunctional. She wondered if she was the only one who sensed this, or if her brothers and sister experienced the same distorted sense of being. She couldn't talk to them or confide in them, nor they her. They all, including Mother and Father, were like empty shells within, and only their anger held the outer surface together. They appeared as walking, talking automatons—neither human nor non-human, just existing.

With another move back into the town of Tuften, the consistent relocating was a singular confirmation that the family was devoid of any permanent roots, values, friendships, or parental consideration of the feelings of the children. The children never knew why it was necessary to move, and to resist would mean beatings or verbal abuse too dreadful to endure. And so, nine months after arriving in Dusty Flats, the family returned to Tuften and a house on Madison Street.

The house on Madison Street had two, big Chinaberry trees in the front yard. Mother sent the children to the tree daily—to supply her with the switches she used for whipping. One time Mother looked at the mangled trees and said that one of them was sure a mess. When she asked what had happened to it one of the boys retorted, "That's the tree you've been sending us to all summer for the sticks to whip us with."

59

That was a big joke for many years. Mother talked about how awful her kids were the summer of the Chinaberry trees. How odd it is to be able to remember something like this that actually may have caused us to laugh. Memories such as those are what most families are made of and I had to work very hard to produce any pleasant recollections. I question, though, Mother's motive for making a joke of that particular incident. Had we been normal, we could have laughed and enjoyed a family anecdote to pass along to our own children. With Mother, I never knew if she was laughing because she truly thought something was humorous, or whether she was being spiteful, insensitive, cruel, or covering up her own unhappiness. Perhaps when I can quit asking myself such questions I can become less critical, and more appreciative of the few stolen moments of laughter from my childhood.

The house had two bedrooms: one for the siblings and the other for the parents. Four children in one bedroom did not bring the youngsters closer emotionally, but created instead a common ground for animosity, jealousy and internal isolation.

I do not remember what my parents' bedroom looked like as we were not allowed into their private domain. As a matter of fact, I cannot remember what any of their bedrooms looked like, in the myriad of homes we found ourselves hidden in over the years of my growing up. This does not puzzle me for it was in those rooms I was taken by Dad when he wanted me to participate in his deviant behavior. It was, and is, too emotionally upsetting to remember, so I do not.

By this time, the father of this sad family was truly buried in the ill effects of alcoholism.

At first I could not remember Dad drinking when we lived on Madison Street. In fact, I didn't really remember him drinking until I was twenty or so. Now, however, when I look back to that house, I can picture him drinking beer.

He was becoming more and more belligerent, hateful, and demanding. Everyone, particularly Mother, was afraid of him.

Wait a minute! What did I just admit to? Mother—afraid? Could it be that she was human, even way back then? Dare I allow her the freedom to feel her own feelings, something which I have insisted she allow me?

It was at the Dusty Flats house where I remember telling my older brother that I hated my mother. He immediately ran to Mother and told her of my disloyalty. Mother has never forgiven me for my childish outburst of emotion; though I'm sure I meant every word at the time. She throws this incident up to me whenever it suits her purpose. I can hear her shrewish voice as I write, "Do you remember screaming at me that you hated me?" Her words are angry, but false, for my brother told her of my tirade—words that were never spoken to her directly. When Joan, my counselor, speaks of selective memory, I finally understand. How much of what I am writing now is selective? Sometimes I wonder about the memory of any of us and how we may or may not mold our pasts to suit whatever emotional needs we have in the present. How can any of us be certain we remember events as they took place?

Another move brought them to a house on Adams Street. By this time people outside the confines of the immediate family were beginning to question and wonder about the goings-on. A resident of the new neighborhood even commented to Mother about how much she spanked her children. Mother, in her usual self-protective demeanor, joked about what the old man had said, making fun of his thick Russian accent. "Can you believe that foreigner questioning what I do with you kids? Why, he doesn't even belong here with his stupid accent I can barely understand. What an idiot!"

Cookie was increasingly aware of her many fears, though not having the capacity or understanding to relate these fears to what was happening to her and being perpetrated upon her. She was particularly afraid of the dark because of the deep aloneness she felt, knowing full well absolutely no one would reach out to her and ease the darkness of her depression.

As I look backward at the littered pathway of my life, the road is dark and I am terrified. My heart speeds up as it did long ago. Mother took me to the doctor then, whose diagnosis was simply that I was a very nervous child. I know that I was afraid of everyone and I'm sure the doctor must have noticed. What bothers me is why he didn't question further for the answer to my timidity and nervous fidgeting. No one ever asked why the little Cookie was so uptight. In my mind's eye that frail little girl looks back at me as if she is now asking me for the answers she never received when her need was the most profound. I guess she and I will find the solution—together.

There were times when Cookie stood at the front door, watching her mother leave for church, purposely without her. It may be ascertained that her plaintive cries could be heard by the surrounding neighbors, as she begged Mother to take her to church, away from Father and the darkness and the pain.

Once more Mother's or Father's words echoed through the hollow parts of my sanity, "If you tell what Daddy is doing to you in the dark, you will be taken away and will never see your family again!" Oh, yes, I was terribly frightened and my rationale convinced me, for the hundredth or thousandth or millionth time, that no matter how bad the abuse was, it must be much worse not to have anyone at all. This thought would somehow sustain me, prepare me and protect me when Mother pretended not to hear my cries as she hurried down the walkway to church. Deborah Miller's words in **Coping With Incest** *burned into my mind: "If the offender is your father, your mother may feel she has little to gain by believing you. If she openly believes you and acts to make her husband leave, she risks losing the economic or emotional security he provides" (118).*

Cookie was left at the mercy of her abusive father's sexual demands.

A different house, a new neighborhood and emotionally, nothing changed—only new methods were devised by Father's insanity to, unwittingly perhaps, provoke the same insanity in his oldest child.

Father's entire existence was bounded by sexual perversion. When Cookie was eleven years old, on Madison Street, he masturbated the dog and made her watch. Also, when the dog or rabbits were bred, he forced her to witness the mating. She was sickened each time, but to refuse to participate meant an extremely severe beating which she was not physically, nor emotionally prepared to suffer. So she withheld her anger and watched and Father was amused, and most likely, sexually aroused.

My father's bizarre methods of receiving sexual pleasure still sicken me, and I find it very hard to understand how he could go through an entire lifetime without the outside world knowing what he was like. Didn't anyone suspect that he was totally deranged and cruelly abusive? It is no wonder so many children are abused and no one outside the family knows. No one pays any attention. This makes me want to cry, not only for myself but for the many others who suffer this secret horror.

The internal pain worsened as Cookie became more aware of the changes within her own body and the way she reacted to what was being done to her. Who could she turn to for answers about what was happening to her body and her attitudes? Innocently she sought answers from one of Father's sisters who had come to live with them at that time. Cookie was blatantly and insensitively chastised, for to ask such questions might expose some of the *secrets* of the family life.

"Such a silly thing to ask—about taking a bath when you are on your period," Mother reproached.

Cookie's aunt said it was okay to ask questions, probably aware that Mother never volunteered any information that pertained to sex in her distorted lack of distinction between sex and gender. To further exacerbate matters, Mother found out about the aunt's willingness to respond. She became extremely angry with her daughter and told her so, making it clear that she was not to be that indiscreet ever again. Family matters were to be kept within the family. Cookie thought it rather strange since she couldn't ask her mother questions about family matters, either. And, after all, her aunt was really family.

There was such an emptiness to life as Cookie entered her 12th year. She was a very tall girl, as compared to others her age, at five foot, six inches and still growing. She was extremely thin, and when she looked in the mirror, the image reflected displeased her. All she could see in that mirror was a stranger with frizzy hair, pimples, long skinny arms and legs, and huge feet. She did not feel related to that person whose sad eyes looked directly back into hers. That replica of her couldn't really be her. That pretense at humanity couldn't be her!

*I am learning, slowly through counseling, that the gangly, awkward, pubescent child was worthy of love, that she deserved to like herself. In Mary Ann Donaldson's booklet, **Incest: Years After**, she states: "Counseling is very painful . . . even more painful than anything you will go through in your life." I must remind myself often of this passage. During some of my most painful times, it helps to keep me going. Someday my life will be restored—the pieces fitting together in a reality of true pleasure and a passion for living. But, it is so difficult.*

Cookie's family reinforced her own negative perceptions about her appearance by constantly telling her how awful she looked, no matter what means she took to look more appealing. As a natural consequence, Cookie felt that to retreat into her own private hell was better than living in the hell called home.

The verbal abuse suffered by Cookie wasn't confined to home. Because of her size, the kids at school found new names to call her, names such as: string bean, toothpick, and skinny Minny. No one, absolutely no one, told her it was okay to be thin. In her distorted view of the world, she began to wonder that if she were fat, she might receive the love she so desperately needed to validate her own existence. The seed of a behavioral change was planted, to grow in the future as compulsion-binge eating.

Years later I discovered that getting fat was not any more effective in gaining the love of those people from whom I so desired. This further established in my mind that I was, indeed, unworthy no matter what I did. My family still treated me badly; a new set of names such as "pig," "fatso," or "oink," had simply replaced the old cruel names. I remember one Thanksgiving Day as an adult, and we were all seated around the table. My youngest brother stared at me, and then started oinking like a pig. Everybody looked at me accusingly. If I said anything and a fight ensued, it would be my fault, not my brother's. I was so upset I couldn't finish my dinner, leaving the table, wondering what they were thinking, yet not wanting to know. It has been ingrained in me, through the years of sexual, verbal and physical abuse, that everyone hides his or her true feelings, and one cannot trust others to be truthful—that to be secretive was to protect oneself from the harsh realities of "What others might think." I catch myself many times during the course of a day, trying to read minds of people I encounter, putting thoughts into their heads as to what they "think about me." It has yet to be driven into my own mind that it really doesn't matter what others think.

It was in Cookie's 12th year that she began her menstrual period. Girls from nurturing, open families most likely had no difficulty making the transition into young womanhood. In Cookie's circumstances, though this may have meant becoming a woman, it brought more inconsistencies of emotion and a new worry where the sexual abuse was concerned.

In her awkward, embarrassed way, Mother told Cookie about her menstrual period, that she would bleed every month, would have to wear a pad, and that was what women did. She made it sound as if being a woman was drudgery and having a menstrual period confirmed the low position in which they were placed. Men did not have to endure such inconvenience and discomfort. It was a tense moment for Cookie and she was relieved when Mother had finished. It was obvious to Cookie that Mother was uncomfortable and not quite sure of her information or how to relate it to her daughter. There was, after the initial explanation, never another discussion about the menstrual period or about sex or any related subject. Mother never asked if Cookie had pain during her period, when it took place, or if she could help. Cookie was left to her own devices in dealing with this new part of her life. The emotional void left by her mother was evidently bottomless.

Father, on the other hand, was continuously probing Cookie for answers to her sexuality and whether she had started her period. Father's questions were deeply personal and Cookie didn't know that she didn't have to respond to his queries into her innermost female secrets. He recognized no boundaries where Cookie was concerned, and there were none he did not try to cross. There was no place for Cookie to hide as Father insisted on knowing all there was to know. He would ask, "Did you notice any blood on your panties?' or, "Are you sure you haven't started your period?" on the day Cookie had fallen on a bike and started to bleed. She was now becoming concerned as to whether she could get pregnant by him.

Each time Dad asked me these questions, I felt as if I had been violated; because of what he had already done to me, his new and worried questions frightened me. I knew he would put something up my vagina, and if his penis could no longer be used, he would use something else, such as a pencil or other object. It angers me to think that he told Mother that I had wanted him to do these things to me—that I asked for it. Am I going to go through the rest of my life being angry with him, and with Mother for allowing the molestation to take place—even though Mother vehemently denies everything? Dear God, I hope not.

Cookie didn't know that father could not have any more children, that he had a vasectomy when they lived in Washington.

When I was a teenager, Mother talked about how she almost died when she had Joyce and could not have any more children, so Dad had been "fixed".

It was during this same year that Cookie decided she no longer wanted to be called Cookie, that the name did not suit her and she never liked it.

When I asked why I had been given the nickname of Cookie I was told that I used to tear up every cake that came into the house.

I don't know why they didn't call me Cake instead of Cookie. Yes. I have a sense of humor, and these past two years of counseling have helped to establish that fact. It feels wonderful to be able to laugh at some of the stupidity and cruelty that took place when I was a child. Could this be part of the healing process? I think it is, if we who have been abused allow it to be so.

Cookie insisted the family use her middle name of Jean; she settled for nothing else. They resisted, but Cookie held her ground, and for the first time in her life the family acquiesced. Jean was born. It would be many years before she became the whole person Jean, but it was a start. The internal void was in the way; Cookie still lived below the outer surface of reality, a protector of a childhood never lived, but yearned for with sadness. Cookie's childhood had been stolen by her parents. She didn't know if her brothers and sister silently lived within the same void.

> **Winged time glides on insensibly, and deceives us; and there is nothing more fleeting than the years.**

> —Ovid

CHILDHOOD PASSES INTO THE LABYRINTH OF DESPAIR

As Jean's female peers were beginning to concern themselves more and more with dating, clothes, best friends, and all the wonderfully worrisome aspects of being a teenager, Jean was hoping for her father's demise. Resentment was building a sturdy foundation for hate. This in turn encouraged the *Bible*-believing young girl to immerse herself in guilt. Still, she spent hours wishing Father would stop hurting her, wishing that she could manifest the courage to just say aloud, "Stop. Leave me alone." Instead she allowed herself to scream the words over and over in her mind. A tiny hope surfaced that maybe Mother would listen—could somehow hear her silent screams. But, no, it was useless. Others had tried to tell Mother of the abuse but she was deaf to all the sadness, turning her back on her child's despair—probably to preserve her own delicate hold on sanity.

If, however, Father died—and Jean wished for this often—he would stop hurting her forever. He deserved the wish to come true. After all, Father's aberration had caused Jean to wish herself dead, why shouldn't he suffer the same ill fate?

God. This hurts so. Why couldn't I have been that little "normal" child I imagined I was—the one who never had to think about scum littering her journey to adulthood? Wait a minute. I can answer that. Several months ago when I began this dissertation I could not have faced such a question with a realistic view. Is this what a psychologist might call a revelation—a breakthrough? Could this be related to hope? Has hope, that one emotion that preserves our world through all its craziness, become a part of my own vocabulary? Yes, it has. When I focus on the child, Cookie, I no longer see a child who was carefree and happy. I envision, instead, a forlorn, tattered little girl who did not smile because she had nothing about which to be happy. It would be detrimental to relive my youth, or to even suppose that I could go back and make things different. I must convince myself of this less often, for there was a time when I just knew my life could be fixed and my mother would be a normal mother and my father would be a perfect father—and my brothers, sister and I could love one another and play and laugh like normal kids. I no longer delude myself. What was, was. It cannot be changed. I can change today. I can even enact change within the perimeters of my being—when I am ready and truly believe I have the ability to control my own life. But, that is the sum total over which I have control. All else is superfluous.

By the time Jean was 14, she and her family had moved to a house on Tuften Highway in the tiny community of Dusty Flats, approximately seven miles from the town of Tuften yet still within the Tuften school district.

The ugliness of Dusty Flats was not only ugly in the eyes of an unhappy teenager. It was grotesquely unsightly from the perspective of most everyone who traveled through its boundaries. A splash of green here and there did not deter one's repulsion to the brown, scorched landscape and it was apparent that snakes and scorpions were the intended occupants of the terrain, being well suited to the dryness.

The family had lived in some pretty awful houses the previous eight years. The place in Dusty Flats was a slight exception. The building had been a dairy in its prime, then converted into a house when the dairy business failed. The bedroom designated for the girls had a consistent moisture build-up, so that at night droplets of water fell upon one of the beds. The entire house had a musty odor which was offensive and impossible to obscure.

Distasteful though it was, the house was larger than the family was accustomed to, allowing the girls their own room separate from the boys and their own bed separate from each other. Finally Jean felt a sense of ownership, with a tiny bit of privacy. The pleasure regarding her good fortune was short lived when it dawned upon her that Father had moved them out of town for a purpose. His reasons were, as always, self-satisfying.

Everything began to come apart at this house. Everyone was so sick.

By then my father was messing around with other women and his meanness grew ever greater beyond reality. We were fighting with one another more often. One time my oldest brother was chasing me and when I hid inside my bedroom with the door closed, he knocked the door off its hinges. The hinges flew from the force of his attack, along with the door lock. When Father and Mother returned from town, my brother and I were beaten without mercy. Another time, same house, my brothers got into a fight. The younger of the two ran into the bathroom and locked the door. The brother in pursuit threw a butcher knife with such anger it went through the bathroom door. Again, both boys were beaten. My older brother was so violent the rest of us children were terribly frightened of him and what he might do. Was he to be another Father, on his way to adulthood and abusive behavior? And what of my younger brother? How did he fit into the picture of copycat behavior? By that time in my life I had learned to listen to whatever I could—to discover what else was taking place within the family. This may have been my natural curiosity, my age, or a survivalist's instinct of preservation.

The ability to control Mother and the children was enhanced by relocating the family to Dusty Flats. Father was the only one who could drive and he was the one who determined whether or not the family traveled into Tuften—or if they deserved an outing. If the children did not behave to Father's satisfaction, they were denied access to church or anywhere else they may have wanted to go.

They had quite a few animals at the dairy-house since it was virtually out in the country. One day while riding, Jean was bucked off her horse. As she lay in the dirt, trying to ascertain whether anything was broken, Mother screamed, "Get up! Get up! You aren't hurt!" She was at least fifty feet away, much too far to determine whether or not Jean was hurt.

Jean wondered how her mother was so sure she wasn't hurt. She felt that Mother didn't care, and it was that attitude which caused the greatest injury and hurt more than the initial pain. Mother's insistence that Jean was unhurt may have been the fear of having to take a trip to the doctor or, more likely, fear of her husband.

Shortly after the horse accident, an old cow pushed Jean into a barbed wire fence. The force of her fall against the barbs caused several deep cuts on both of her legs. From that day forward she was afraid of cows and horses. It was not a normal, respectful fear—the kind of fear that keeps people from putting themselves in dangerous situations. Jean became physically ill if she thought she would be placed in a pen with either animal.

The magnification of Jean's fears surely was caused by a lack of nurturing, but Jean's problem went far beyond the lack of parental or sibling bonding. Her fears were invisible so she felt as if she was being tortured from within where no one could see what was happening. Her perceptions of the world were limited due to youth, inexperience, and her aloneness. She had no idea how to control her fears, or even if they were, in fact, controllable. She had no one with whom she could share her concerns. It would be years down her littered highway before she learned, with the help of her therapist, that many of the fears were a direct result of the sexual abuse.

Jean was going through her transition from childhood to womanhood, and it was during this phase she began to question what was, and had been, happening to her. Furthermore, she was becoming more analytical in regard to her parents' behavior. She was completely aware that her father controlled the family's life with a steel-like grip that seemed to squeeze the emotional life from everyone who lived in his house. In this depraved kingdom of his making, the only opinions of any value were his own. When questioned about his authority or his behavior, he became violent.

I remember one time when Mother dared to stand up to Dad. He hit her with his fist, giving her a black eye. I cannot recall her ever challenging him again. He was the brutal force of authority and should be treated with respect and fear. Ha! As if any one of us considered respect. Fear far outweighed the normal feelings children generally associated with the term Father. Could he have been so deluded to think of himself as a god of some kind?

From the time Jean was 13 until she was 15 Father attempted to rape her. Several times when he tried to force his penis into her, Jean cried out in pain. She was sure he stopped because he was afraid someone would hear her cries. Nevertheless, he was going to do what he desired and in his perverse insanity, he stuck pencils inside of her vagina. He knew, instinctively and sadistically, the indignity and shame he placed upon his daughter. He treated Jean and his other children as possessions, not people.

Uncle J, Mother's half-uncle, came to live with the family. Some weeks after his arrival, Uncle J was caught peeking at Jean and her sister while they were taking showers. Father was furious and ran him off their property and down the road. Obviously it was acceptable to commit incest upon his own child, but it was not acceptable by anyone else.

I thought then how hypocritical this seemed. Actually, it involved his possession of me, as if I was an inanimate object to be owned. After all, objects don't hurt or feel. Perhaps he thought I was expendable and without emotion, and even though he needed me for his perversion I could be discarded like playthings to be put back in a cupboard when play time was over. I realize this now, but when I was being molested I thought I was the only one. I could not imagine that any other family member was suffering his own trauma at the hands of Father's perversity. I learned years later, that Father's deviant behavior was most likely not restricted to just me. All those many years I had thought I had been singled out by my father. Mother obviously told Father about my accusations because I received a severe beating. I remember there being a fight, but I didn't know why. I was suffering too deeply to acknowledge anyone's pain but my own.

The damage to Jean's psyche was almost complete and why she had not done herself in or committed patricide was a puzzle to be confronted in her later years. The thought of doing both, or having both done by some outside force, were close to Jean's consciousness yet she never acted on her anger.

Dissecting and rearranging my childhood became a hobby of mine during my teenage years. It was like a game. I would concentrate on the harm that had been done to me by my father and then by my mother. I would focus on the hurt and, I'm sure, must have derived some pleasure feeling sorry and sad for myself and about my fate in life. These games that I played with my mind were all I had to grasp and call my very own. It was perverse, perhaps, but those memories gave me something to attach myself to. I feel they may have saved my sanity, my life, and the life of my father. My friend, many times, has said, "I don't know what kept you from committing murder. I'm sure I would have wiped both your parents off the face of the earth had I been the child in question." Easy to say when one is not the victim. Looking at this passage as I write, I feel my games provided my defense, my armor, and my survival. That was what I had. That was what I relied upon to carry me through one abusive episode after another.

Jean did not know that she had rights to feel angry and sad, or to hate what her father continued to do. She did not know it was okay to even hate her mother for condoning the brutal behavior of her father. She was never allowed to voice an opinion or express a feeling. She felt helpless and frustrated.

Sadness overwhelmed her when she felt unloved or alone, which was often.

She had no place to hide or get away from all the pain. She never had a room by herself, a private place safe from her father's eyes or ears. Father would listen in on her phone calls. He read what she had written. He had total disregard for her privacy, at times sharing what he had discovered with the rest of the family, embarrassing Jean because Father made her appear stupid, and thus, she felt stupid.

What I didn't realize was that Father's acts of unkindness were not a reflection on my inadequacies. They could have been a cover-up for his guilt if he ever felt any, or an indication of his mental impotence. If I allow myself to picture one of those occasions where he cruelly tried to discredit me, I should be able to snub my nose at the fool, for only a fool wastes his time trying to make others appear foolish, particularly children who are defenseless. Maybe someday the tears will dry and the memories will recede into the nightmare that was my childhood, to be filed away in my wellness. It is much too early in my therapy. I am not ready because so much wreckage still litters the roadway to my safe house.

The family was seated in the living room. Jean—head bowed in her usual position as if hoping not to be noticed—was 15 years old. Her sister, who was nine at the time, looked at Jean, and for reasons unknown except to the child herself, said, "You're so ugly and skinny no one in the world will ever love you." Stunned, Jean looked up, first at her sister then her mother. Tears behind her eyelids threatened to trickle down her reddened cheeks.

Mother sat in abject silence, neither coming to Jean's defense, nor acknowledging the younger sister's cruel statement with a kind look in Jean's direction. There she sat, in her rigidity, a breathing, emotionally dead, human being. An opportunity had presented itself for this mother to substantiate her older daughter's worth and existence but she sat mute, her face devoid of emotion. One can only hope that it was fear of retribution from the father that kept this woman from nurturing or defending her child. To imagine otherwise could lead one to believe that the mother actually hated the teenager, finding her bothersome, unworthy and appropriately denigrated.

My friend and co-author has insisted, since the very beginning of this book, that my father most likely raped my mother, causing her first pregnancy—me. In the 1940s and 1950s, most girls would marry to avoid the scandal of an unwed pregnancy and subsequent birthing of a bastard child. Mother may have blamed me for all of her unhappiness. After all, had she not been forced to marry, her life would not have become the maelstrom of abuse and unhappiness that it had. Rather than focus on the rape of her body and soul, and place the blame where it belonged, on Father, Mother chose to transfer all of her hatred onto me. It makes a hapless kind of sense, but learning the truth is far away. Mother will never admit to anything so ugly, so full of shame being perpetrated upon her. Her conscious mind may have forced the memory of my beginning far back into her mind—so far as to never be reached again. Yet, I cannot help but wonder if my friend is correct in her assessment, and I cannot but hope that I will one day know the absolute truth as unrealistic as this may seem.

Jean remained silent out of self-preservation. Had she expressed her feelings, she would have been ridiculed because obviously the truth had been spoken, and she would have been slapped across the face with force—sadly, with pleasure. The other children would have witnessed the event with relief that the anger of Mother and Father was directed at their sister, not them. And Jean, with the torture of unshed tears squashing her ego further into the pit of depression, truly believed that she was stupid, ugly, and unlovable. Furthermore, if her family did not love her, no one ever would.

The subject of that particular incident was repeated many times during my youth, in more subtle ways. In my later years I questioned Mother as to why she hadn't defended me, assuming she was aware of my delicate emotional state at 15. She became quite angry, insisting that she would never have allowed my sister to talk to me in such a way. I know Mother immediately contacted my sister after she had spoken to me because of what took place an hour later. My sister called, screaming, "I never did such a thing. You have a big imagination, Jean." She hung up. Maybe I had misinterpreted the episode. How would I ever know unless Mother and my sister were willing to discuss the matter? How could I begin to understand the craziness of my family if no one was willing to talk about what bothered them. I felt as if I was constantly banging my head against an impenetrable wall which surrounded my family and trapped them inside a structure of mental and physical depravity. No matter how hard I struggled to force that wall to come tumbling down, they all held fast within their sickness and fear. With the help of my therapist, I was learning that my family's cruelty and insensitive put-downs were not directed at me because I was all those ugly, bad things they vocalized. It was directed at me as a defense mechanism against their own inadequacies, their self-proclaimed guilt, and their need to appear normal by making me appear abnormal. I was a scapegoat simply because I was in their presence as a family member and I was easily victimized. It saddens me deeply to think back to the "you're ugly, no one will ever love you" incident, but at least now I know the problem was more theirs than mine. I was not ugly. I not only could receive love, I could give it. In the second year of therapy my emotional burden was becoming lighter as I discarded more of my own insecurities and placed them in the garbage where they belonged—almost as if I was sweeping the litter from the road to wellness. It was my hope that my Mother would eventually accept the fact that I was a real person, with real feelings and that I had value. I was still deluded by the thought that she, too, could become well if I did, and she would praise me for my courage, although I have read: ". . . moms of abused kids often carry around a sense of injustice, of being victimized, and a sense of helplessness . . ." ("Hidden Victims" 18).

Had the 15 year old Jean known what her future held, she may have determined that it looked so gloomy, and her problems so irresolvable, that to self-destruct was the only reasonable solution. Instead, she pushed the pain down, down into her already ravaged soul by avoidance. Sometimes, however, the pain could not be ignored, would surface and grip Jean's outward self with abandon. Tears would flow freely at those times, unbidden, with the promise of cleansing her soul. The tears, of course, did not cleanse completely for Jean would turn from tearful, to argumentative, to combative. She fought with her brothers and sister to hide the true feelings of pain. Had she expressed how she truly felt she would have been punished. If her mother said, "Shut up" and Jean replied, "Okay," Mother would take Jean by the hair and bang her head against the wall or slap her repeatedly on the face. Though the expression "Okay" does not seem to be an expression of how this young girl felt, she was punished for saying it nonetheless. Then, as if manipulated by puppet strings, Mother would slink away, withdrawing into her own shell of silence. Jean was endlessly left standing with her emotional sores festering, never being allowed to heal. The wounds were consistently and consciously reopened by Mother's own psychological brutality. "There are three types of mothers in incest families: those who genuinely don't know, those who may know, and those who do know. The final type is the most reprehensible: the mother who is told of the molestation by her children and does nothing about it" (Forward 158).

THE SEXUAL ABUSE
ENDS ABRUPTLY

Jean did not know how many tears she shed during her teenage years. It seemed as if she was always crying, always sad, and always alone and lonely. Her tears were a way of reaffirming her validity as a person. Surely if one could cry, one had some worth, beyond the self-sorrow. She wondered where God was during these times. Did He not see her tears? She thought of herself as a good girl who worshipped and obeyed God as she had been taught.

When Jean started high school, she carried her *Bible* with her every day, everywhere. Whether this gesture was established as a proof to God that she was good was not a conscious thought, but she did feel that it protected her from the world. The *Bible* was a threatening tome and Jean believed that everyone feared the wrath of God. By creating a visible barrier she would be safe.

Though Jean questioned her God many, many times during a week, particularly those times when Father was his most abusive, she felt that if she could prove her dedication to God and the church, she would someday be released from her earthly hell. It was at this time, when she was 15, that she began watching the people at church and listening to what they were saying. The pain pierced ever further into her being.

She learned that it was a sin to show anger. Jealousy of her siblings was wrong.

She learned about guilt and shame and felt both when she associated them with what her parents were doing to her, especially her father. The more she learned the more she wanted to know, and she watched and listened for answers which might inadvertently come her way.

She discovered that many of the people who professed righteousness were not good people. Some stated beliefs, loud and profound, and yet acted entirely different when outside the church. They were uncaring and made things worse by their gossip about the family and the problems with Mother and Father's marriage. When kindness would have helped so much, many church members thought themselves better than Jean's family and "tsk-tsked" rather than show compassion to the children. Jean was sad and extremely angry with the people whom she felt should have cared.

Still, Jean was very much involved in the church youth activities and programs. She was a member of the choir and thoroughly enjoyed going to other churches in town to sing. Singing Christian music was one of the few activities sanctioned by the church. Members were not allowed to go to the movies or to dances. The female members were not allowed to wear lipstick or pants. Even with the restrictions, Jean enjoyed her church involvement and felt as if she belonged with the youth group. It provided her with a reason to stay away from the activities at school.

Jean did not date during this period of her life, although other girls her age were exploring the world of relationships with delight, deliciously self-inflicted emotional trauma, and eagerness. Jean was anxious about male-female relationships and commitments. Her anxiety pushed her away from others in high school. Her fear of men isolated her and only her *Bible* protected her. She did not care that other kids called her churchified and found her inaccessible. She preferred it that way for it was easier to deal with than the lack of trust she had for the boys her age. Because of her own sexually abusive background, she was convinced that all males had only sex on their minds and the word itself generated pictures of disgust and fear in her mind.

A friend asked me if I ever had fun being a teenager, or if I had girlfriends with whom I could sit, laugh and talk. "No," I replied to her query, "not really." My one friend and I took turns visiting one another but we spent our time playing Monopoly, not discussing what was going on secretively within our families. I didn't know that she was being sexually molested. I did know her mother spanked her on a rather consistent basis, for behavior her mother found irritating, regardless of its actual severity. Sometimes it was simply a childish act that a normal parent may have found amusing and forgivable.

It is evident to me today that we gravitated toward one another because of our similar lifestyles, our internal pain, and our daily emotional trauma. Though our reasons for being friends in the beginning may not have been normal, we needed each other. We served as distinct, survival tools for one another. But, no, we didn't giggle and share boy secrets or compare articles of clothing to decide what to wear to school. The only laughter I remember that we shared was one evening when we were doing dishes at her house. My friend had taken the sponge she was using for the dishes, bent down and washed her dog's nose, then continued to wash the dishes with the same sponge. We found the incident hilarious and I glory still at the memory of that laughter.

Sometimes when I went by my friend's house on the way to school, I would be crying. Her mother tried to soothe me, as if she found my life unfair. Perhaps she was projecting her own guilt into the unhappiness she saw in me. I did not understand her empathy for me when I knew she was being mean to her own daughter in a way similar to what my mother was doing to me, my brothers and sister.

I know I missed something quite remarkable in the growing up process. It was as if I went from birth to adulthood in a single moment, without any of the necessary, positive emotional aspects that help people to become responsible, caring adults who have an understanding of normal behavior and normal relationships.

Nor can I remember walking or running in the rain with my friend, laughing as we sought refuge, yet not really caring if we were soaked clear through our clothes to our skin. What a laugh. Had either one of us fallen prey to such a wonderfully exquisite, youthful delight, we would have suffered consequences neither of us was willing to suffer.

I remember raindrops upon my cheeks that were not raindrops, but the never—ending tears of a child who grew up too fast because her father forced sex upon her when she lay in a crib, barely a year old. I remember raindrops that came through rooftops in houses where we lived—houses that weren't fit for humans or for beasts of burden, only rats, bats and other disgustingly ugly creatures of the dark.

I don't remember the tears burning behind my eyelids the day I told my father to stop the sexual abuse, but I am sure they existed. I was 15 years old at the time.

Jean was terrified that the perversion would last forever and that thought frightened her beyond the fear of Father's wrath. In the vernacular of today, Jean had had it. The sexual abuse had to stop and it was evident to her that she must be the one to deal with the perversity of Father. She had no other ally within the family, and she dared not approach anyone outside the family.

For a time, Jean avoided her father as much as possible. If she were unavailable, she couldn't be used. The rest of the children were avoiding him also. No one wanted to go anywhere with Father, nor did anyone wish to be alone with him in the house.

Father was becoming more and more upset with the children for evading him, and their refusal to go anywhere alone with him must have caused him great concern. What was happening to the control he had exerted over them all for so long a time? The insanity of his behavior, and the obsession of his desire to be the absolute ruler of his domain, did not allow him to see the reasoning behind the children's evasive maneuvers. He may simply have assumed they were being disobedient.

The day came when Jean, her anger leading her into the dangerous realm of this disobedience, and with total resolution, informed her father, "Leave me alone or you'll be in big trouble." Jean and her father were standing in the hallway. He looked at his daughter without saying a word, turned and walked away. The sexual abuse ended that very day—against Jean. It can be presumed that her father did not discontinue his aberrant sexual practices. A sex offender does not rehabilitate him/herself in a moment—if ever.

Her unhappiness did not stop as she had hoped nor did her tears go away. They tragically began to express a different pain, a different desperation.

When I was a child, I had no power.
When I spoke, no one heard me.
My voice was too weak and tentative
to have an effect. Even though I am
an adult now, I still feel powerless to
affect change at times.

From: *Affirmations For The Inner Child*
—Rokelle Lerner

TRANSFERENCE

Looking at the future through the eyes of a 15 year old, Jean could only imagine that life had to get better. It certainly couldn't get any worse. The sexual attacks inflicted upon her by Father had ceased, and Jean saw a tiny ray of hope lighting the road to adulthood. Had she, with some sort of prophetic vision, known what was before her, she may have opted to terminate at age 15.

I vaguely remember feeling a sense of relief that my father took my threat seriously, that he would be in deep trouble if he didn't leave me alone. I'm trying hard to recall if I didn't also feel a bit of power—a sense of control over this man who had controlled me so viciously for so long. Could that fleeting feeling of power have prompted my strong desire to survive beyond and above what was happening to me? Is that why I didn't swallow pills or put a gun to my head and end my life? The possibility may have existed, but at the time my conscious elation was short-lived. Father stopped the sexual abuse, but the emotional abuse worsened.

Jean's father had been, we can suppose, thrown off balance by Jean's outburst of defiance and independence. He became the tyrant about whom books are written, and about whom psychologists and psychiatrists may puzzle over as they hear story after story of men such as this inhumane person who dominated his family into complete submission, physically, emotionally and spiritually—as perpetuated by TV programs such as *Law and Order SVU*. His craziness boiled over the top of an emotional cauldron which had no lid. Cruelty and abasement flowed freely with no boundaries or containment—ergo, no rules. He couldn't be talked to nor approached in any positive manner. He developed an insane possessiveness of all his children, controlling every nuance of defiance or independence. Hell had moved in bag and baggage and, like an unwanted relative, refused to depart once settled within the receiving family's domain.

Outside of murdering the man, before any more damage could be done to the psyche of Jean, there seemed no other recourse but compliance.

Although the oldest son battled with everyone else within the family, Jean was the most fearful of her father. To her, Brother's aggressive, angry behavior seemed a shield against the pain she thought he must have felt, the confusion and frustration of all the insane messages being received. These messages were from a father who knew nothing better than how to inflict indignity upon indignity, demeaning and demoralizing his family. A child may find it difficult to love when fear blocks out other emotions. All that may be left of an abused youth was genuine hatred, guilt because of the hatred, and a strong need for nurturing that s/he knew, deep within his/her soul, would never, ever be part of life. As a result, a child acts out his anger, perhaps as the display artist, the method actor, the "exposé" of the family's dysfunction.

*Paradoxically, I laugh as this is being written. My father had a stroke some weeks ago and is lying in a hospital bed, mostly paralyzed and barely alive. My oldest brother, to me always the aggressor, fawns over Dad's limp body as if guarding it from intruders (which, naturally, include me). He dramatizes the role of the devoted son, reading the **Bible** in a loud, strong voice and I wonder whether this is to impress the hospital staff or again, to hide the family secrets so that the finger of shame would not be pointed at any of us. To me, he portrays the loving son in this bizarre and obvious life-drama, as if he were on a stage and expects at any moment that the audience will break into a standing ovation.*

But, if the phoniness of the script is obvious to me, I would think it obvious to those who don't even know us. In my eyes, this man is playing the part of the fool—not the emotional son who mourns his father's illness. How sad that he cannot, or chooses not to, understand this foolish role he plays, and that it has no value to a family that has no value.

As I watched my brother, I wanted to denounce his actions by telling him, "The world is not listening, Brother Dear, nor is it looking at us or inside our lives. It does not care. We are nothing to this imaginary world we have created in our heads, and for whom we perform because we believe it to be expected of us. Stop playing the stupid games, take off your disguise, and face the reality of a childhood that went all wrong and which has since spilled over into a dysfunctional and crazy adulthood. We may be actors upon the stage of life, but the people you may be trying to fool—the world outside the family—walked out of the theater long ago. Once again Dr. Susan Forward's words reaffirm what I was feeling at that moment: "Incest victims often become very skillful child actors. In their inner world there is so much terror, confusion, sadness, loneliness, and isolation that many develop a false self with which to relate to the outside world, to act as if things were fine and normal" (156). Only we were children no more.

When Jean's oldest brother was 16 he met a young woman in church, three years his senior. The two quickly became a couple and seemed completely devoted to one another. The girl graduated from high school, moved to a new location to begin a job, leaving her boyfriend alone and devastated at her departure from his life. He soon began skipping school to visit his girl in order to continue their relationship. When Mother and Father discovered their son was truant and why, they tried to forbid him from ever seeing the young lady again. This son, who was very vocal and aggressive, fought with his parents for permission to marry when the girl became pregnant. He needed his parent's signatures because he was underage. Mother, in an unusual move, sided with her child and said she would agree. She believed the two should marry for the sake of the unborn child. Father adamantly refused to release his son from his control and the battle that ensued caused the boy to drop out of school, leave his father's domain and join the Navy.

The youngest son, quite the opposite of his brother, was completely internal by the time he and Jean entered into and proceeded through their teen years. He never voiced his feelings, desires, or opinions. No one knew what he was thinking, nor what action he would take. He appeared to take everything in stride, to adjust, and to comply because he did not give any outward display of what he was thinking.

The younger son appeared to have learned the lessons and the necessity of secretiveness better than any of the other children. At age 15 he began dating a young girl who was very much like he: secretive, outwardly unemotional, and wary. In May of their 18th year, and just prior to high school graduation, he and his girlfriend were married.

Twenty-eight years have gone by since my younger brother's wedding. He is still married to the same person, both of them still presenting with the demeanor of high school: reserved, non-committal, and outwardly unemotional. He has stated that he doesn't have a problem with life, and yet I can't help but wonder . . . How do he and his wife remain so rigid? Are they trying to convince the world, with their sullenness, that they aren't emotional messes? Am I being too judgmental when I see their adult children, on the other hand, having visible problems and I think it must be the fault of the parents?

When I was at the hospital the other day, visiting my father, my youngest brother brushed by me with a muffled, "Hello." He sat with Dad for a short time, not uttering more than a word or two, then left as quietly as he had come. Nothing had changed. We will never be normal even when Dad is dead. We are not kindred spirits—only kin.

By the time Jean was ready to enter college at age 19, the family had managed to keep its secrets from the world while destroying each individual personality. They were emotional cripples without a clue as to what direction they should take for their sanity, their productivity, or their continued existence in a life cloaked in secrecy. For Jean, entering college, away from the ugly walls of her room, a sense of freedom may have momentarily motivated her to extend her horizons beyond the small town in which she suffered so much pain. Along with this new freedom, fear of the unknown traveled in close accordance.

Her sense of inadequacy was also her companion. Father's influence had far reaching effects no matter how far away she moved, because the emotional foundation had been established in her childhood. The second stage of Jean's life was taking shape. Even though she was no longer a child, Cookie the abused child still lived deep within her. Indeed, her innocence had been stolen, yet her ability to deal with life at the adult level was non-existent. Jean soon discovered that life was hell and getting worse. The Secret remained in her soul, and without her knowledge continued to dictate her responses to her world.

PART II

PAST AND PRESENT COLLIDE

The veil which covers the
face of futurity is woven
by the hand of mercy.

—Bulwer

HOPE WANES

High school graduation, 19—, was a time of high excitement
for the young students receiving their diplomas in Tuften.
They possessed the dreams of youth, and the energy to go
forward into the world and become grown-up people, separate
from parental authority. Even Jean felt somewhat happy as her
future plans included going to a Bible College in Costa Mesa,
California. There she would finally be out from under the
dictates of her father and mother, and could forget her past
pain. She could go forward into a state that she had never
before found herself—the state of absolute freedom.

With childish hope, I thought it to be so easy to rid myself of
my past once I was gone from my destructive environment. I had
nothing on which to base this assumption, but it seemed to me a real
solution to my unhappiness. Had I any vision of the future, I think
that I would have given up entirely. Today I am thankful that I had
no inkling that matters had to become much worse before I could be
free of the emotional cripple who was me at age 19.

As a graduation gift from high school, Father presented
Jean with a $100.00 savings bond. She was surprised and
thought the money hers, that she could use it for college
education. Father, however, said that Jean could not cash the
bond, that she must keep it until it matured. Jean's momentary
pleasure passed as she realized that her father, once again, had
managed to exercise his control over her. The gift took on a
different meaning—icy, inflammable matter snuffing out the

fire that had been ignited at the prospect of going away to school.

That summer, prior to entrance into college, Jean baby sat two children who were from a divorced family. The children lived with their father, Jacob, a man 33 years old, stocky and balding. Soon after her job began, Jacob asked Jean for a date. Jean was not accustomed to attention from a man other than her father. Dating seemed as remote to her as freedom from her home life.

For a brief six weeks, Jean's life took on the appearance of normalcy. She was part of a process of growing in which young women learn to be selective about future mates—a time of physical and emotional awareness of bodies and their effect upon the opposite sex.

As with many young couples in a new relationship, the dating involved dinner out, swimming at the local pool, and cruising (a common, fairly inexpensive past time during that era). Jean, however, had a nagging doubt about Jacob. She could not disassociate his motives from those of her father. In her mind, all men were conscientiously bent on hurting her—using her body for perverse, sadistic pleasures. Thus far, she had only encountered men of one type and she was suspicious, though not outwardly so. She expected this new man in her life to be aggressive and demanding, without concern for her needs, as her father had been.

Eventually the relationship evolved into more than Jean was ready to accept. Jacob told her he wanted a sexual relationship, though he did not love her. Having been married, and used to sex on a somewhat regular basis, Jacob was expressing his needs. Jean was impressed with his honesty, but did not, under any circumstances, desire to become sexually active with him. She refused his advances, yet Jacob accepted the refusal in a gentlemanly way—something totally opposite of what her father would do. Perhaps a small glimmer of hope arose in the young woman that not all men were as her father. Maybe she could find happiness in a normal male-female union.

With what seemed an uncanny ability, Father suspected that Jean's relationship with Jacob had gone beyond employer-employee. Most likely, because of his own sexual perversion, he thought all men to be as he. His property was being sexually exploited by another man, and he was jealous beyond control, and certainly beyond the boundaries of an emotionally healthy father. There was no other reason for his behavior when he arrived at Jacob's home one day, in a psychotic rage, and literally dragged Jean by the arm out the front door. During the time he held firmly onto Jean, Father was cursing at Jacob and shouting, "You had better stay away from my daughter or I'll beat the crap out of you!"

I felt humiliated, embarrassed, and deeply angry. I knew, without a doubt, that a normal relationship with a man would never be easy, if ever possible. When Father and I arrived home that day, I went into the bedroom and cried for what seemed like hours. I had no idea that I had any rights in the situation, that I was legally considered an adult and had choices that I could have made. Furthermore, I did not realize that I was burying the new hatred of my father with that which already existed. So I cried my tears, dried my tears, and never saw Jacob again—because that is what my father expected of me, and I complied. Now, with the help of my therapist, I know that I was collecting bits of emotional garbage, and strewing it in my pathway to maturity.

For the remainder of the summer, Jean prepared for her trip to Costa Mesa and a new way of life. Although she was fearful of being on her own, in a different setting, she was secretly eager to leave Tuften and all it symbolized.

I believe, in retrospect, that I experienced an internal, pleasant excitement, an emotion that was formerly obscured by all the savagery that had been inflicted upon me. I think that I also feared if my father suspected I was eager to leave, he would have forbid me to go. And, he must have experienced some fear, himself—that I would expose the family secret, or possibly that I would become sexually active with other men. I have learned, through counseling, those men such as my father experience much anxiety in regard to protecting the Secret and in maintaining absolute control over the family.

As the date to leave for college became closer, it was apparent to Jean that she would have to ask her father's help with the financial burden. When she did so, his reply was a resounding "No! You'll have to get a job and stay here!"

My worst fears were realized. I could feel my hopes being dashed against the rocks of my despair. Then, I did something which surprised even me . . .

Jean, bitterly angry but undaunted, took a stance against her father by cashing in the savings bond he had given as a graduation gift.

Part of my salvation, today, must have begun at that very moment, for to rebel against Father was not my normal behavior. I can imagine that Father became extremely anxious when he learned that I had gone against his wishes, and that thought is very stimulating!

Two weeks late for her departure to college because of her financial difficulties—which were resolved by cashing in her bond—Jean was finally packed and ready to catch the bus to southern California. Her father was lying down in his bedroom, recalcitrant as a small child and refusing to acknowledge Jean's departure. Jean walked into his bedroom, quietly stating she was ready to leave. He said not a word, as if she were not even there. She picked up her suitcases and walked out the front door of the house.

I'm not sure what I expected my father to do or say that day I left for school. Whatever I may have expected, he did not alter his predictable behavior in any way. He dismissed me from his life, as he dismissed everything he was finished using—by totally ignoring its existence. What was going on in his mind could only be conjecture on my part. Or wishful thinking.

It was September, two weeks into the term, when Jean got off the bus to begin her college career. She was scared and unsure as to what was expected of her in the new surroundings. It was her first time without Father programming her actions and reactions, and though she was glad he was not there to direct her, she was frightened because she had never been taught the proprieties of living outside her cloistered existence. It was difficult for her to believe or accept the fact that she was alone—totally detached from the family. The feeling was neither good nor bad, but during her entire stay in Costa Mesa, Jean did not miss the presence of her family at all.

Unfortunately, her college days were not to provide the necessary distance from her father. Slowly and insidiously, he insinuated himself and his insanity into her new environment. What hope she had of being free from emotional bondage was short-lived.

Beware of jealousy,
It is the green-eyed monster which doth mock
The meat it feeds on.

—Shakespeare

THERE ARE NO FAIRY TALES

The young woman who walked into the dorm room was the same who had walked away from her family in Tuften. The emotional barriers she had formed around herself in order to insulate her from any more pain were firmly in place. Jean was scared of these new surroundings, but in her heart she felt a sense of excitement that filled her with hope. It was this excitement that she wished others to respond to, but they could not see past the barriers of Jean's pain. Her new roommate, Bonnie, was a tiny thing who excelled in many areas, especially in academics and music. She did not appear to have many friends, but she was friendly and open and Jean felt comfortable being her "roomie". At the beginning of their association, Bonnie was responsive to Jean, but as time passed, Jean's dependency on their friendship became a burden. Jean, who had never really been exposed to the vagaries of friendship, did not realize that she was smothering Bonnie with too much attention, too much dependency. Jean needed the closeness of a best friend; Bonnie did not.

*What I really needed, way back then, was a therapist, and I suppose I was trying to put my roommate in that position. In fact, I was totally ignorant that help could be found in the form of a counselor, and part of that ignorance was born of the fact that I was not allowed to expose **The Secret**. Times have changed, yet many, many young people do not know that there are options for them, that they can get the needed help. Had I been able to appeal* to someone when I first entered college, I would have been spared the next 20+ years of emotional pain, grief, anger, repressed hate, and confusion that directed my life.

Most likely Bonnie sensed, rather than verbalized, Jean's many needs. She could not respond to those needs, however, nor fulfill them. Jean felt Bonnie pushing her away emotionally, but could not understand why she affected people in this way. It seemed to happen each time she made friends. The barriers and defenses, though not visible as a physical entity, were visible to the senses of those with whom she came in contact.

Now that I am part of group therapy, I can see those barriers in many of the members, as they have told me of my own. It is amazing to me how each of us defends our survival in such different ways—some outwardly functioning as normal, law-abiding citizens, while others fall prey to openly aggressive behavior of a psychotic, anti-social nature. Who or what determines this factor up in our brains? I have known or read about people with similar backgrounds as mine who defy the laws of man and nature with aberrant behavior. We read about these people daily in our newspapers as they are being sentenced to jail for murder and/or mayhem. On the other hand, people such as my brothers, sister and I obey the laws of our society—at least to the casual observer. God only knows what dishonesties my family may have perpetrated which were punishable by the law, but were never discovered by the law!

Jean's chance at friendship was thwarted by her own behavior and she was unaware of the reasons why. In her mind, she felt unworthy because of her inability to form close attachments, and she spent much time mentally berating herself. That she was not free from her past was becoming painfully apparent.

Her father substantiated this fear by imposing his existence into her space at the Bible college the second month she was there.

By October Jean was fully ensconced in the routine of her classes and doing reasonably well. Her personal relationships weren't faring equally, but she had learned to accept rejection as a given because of her feelings of unworthiness. She enjoyed learning and managed to secure decent grades in spite of her distress. Then, her hope of escape reached a new low with the arrival of her parents for their first visit.

Jean was unprepared for what took place that October day in Costa Mesa. Her parents arrived together, but soon after her mother disappeared to leave father and daughter alone to discuss a family matter.

I have yet to discover what happened to Mother that day—where she went or what she did. I remember wondering why she would leave me alone with my father, but I did not question his authority.

With Mother out of the way, Father took Jean to lunch at a rather refined restaurant. It was there, while the two were eating, that he dropped the mind-destroying bomb. With aplomb, Jean's father told her of an illicit affair in which he was then involved. He detailed every movement of the affair, complete with how many times a day he and his lover, whom he identified, performed the sex act. He spared no adjective, describing the relationship as the voyeur he was, and aroused his own sexuality as his words flowed easily from his tongue. As he spoke, his eyes penetrated his daughter's, looking for her response to his confession. That he enjoyed himself was obvious to Jean. Why he enjoyed himself was outside her ability to understand.

I could not believe he would do this to me, or to my mother! I cannot remember what I was eating. I only recall that after Father had confessed his adultery with such pleasure, I ate very little. I had no appetite for food, nor for the man sitting across from me pretending to be my father. He was so sick! My first emotion was total and absolute anger. I did not want to hear what he was saying. I could not scream at him as I wanted. We were, after all, in a public place and we had been taught never to display anything in public. He was so smugly secure. I am certain that was the reason he told me in a restaurant rather than back at my dorm room. The pleasure he achieved from telling me was disgusting, and I was so mortified that all I could do was cry. I think he knew that, too. He may have been (and continued to be until his death a few weeks ago) crazy, but he was not stupid. He had me right where he wanted me, knowing how I would feel, knowing how I would react. After all, he had programmed me. Not only was he deriving sick, sexual pleasure, he managed to lower me to the depths of his own perversity by being so detailed about his affair. My friend has suggested another interesting reason as to his motive for doing what he did—jealousy. He may have thought that by telling me of an affair I would be jealous and willing to be taken home to prevent him from falling prey to another woman's wiles. He may have been jealous of the imagined lovers I might take while in college. It is obvious to my friend that he wanted, and somehow needed, my presence in his life and that in his sickness, he loved me as a man loves a woman, not as a father loves a daughter. The whole incident, and the memory of it, sickens me for whatever reasons he may have had.

As easily as Father had declared his adultery, he returned Jean to her dorm and left for Tuften. He had come and conquered, destroyed and defiled. We can be certain that Jean was left more of an emotional cripple than before, and more under the influence of her father's evil than she ever thought possible. Would there ever be an end to such horror? Jean could no longer hope for freedom. No matter how far away she went, Father's image would follow, dictate, control.

The restaurant scene was repeated more than once through phone communication. Jean's father called and bragged about the woman with whom he was committing adultery. Father's actions made little sense to Jean, or to anyone else in the family. By Thanksgiving of that year, everyone knew of Father's infidelity—the family, and the townspeople who found delight in gossip and someone else's pain and sadness.

My father's mistress was considered White Trash, even in the poorest sections of town. She was only six years older than I, and 13 years younger than my father. She had been married a couple of times by the time Dad had his affair with her. She began having children at 14 or so, and the year of her affair with my father, she was already the mother of 13 children of varying ages—13 poor lost souls who ran around dirty and wild and sad. That Dad would call to brag about this poor, wretched creature who was the brunt of the town's dislike and wrath, was another sign of the sickness that resided up in his head. Perhaps he felt his actions would degrade all of us, especially mother and me, even further, and that was his desire—to drive us deeper into the pits of hell. We certainly shall never know, now that my father lies within the confines of a coffin, unable to communicate. And even if he were able, I doubt that he would attach any meaning or importance to what happened so many years ago. He never had faced the reality of his insanity while living. Somehow, I feel cheated because he died before I could force him to be normal—as if anyone could accomplish such a miracle.

The calls began, supposedly caring people from the church the family attended. They all knew! The gist of the calls consisted of: "Do you know what your dad is doing?" and "Do you know how upset your mother is?" As if Jean had any control over what was taking place at home, the calls continued to the point where Jean wanted to scream, "Shut up and leave me alone!" She knew their concern was masking malicious meddling. They were as sick as her family! She no longer could deal with this mess alone and knew that if she did not get help soon, she would go mad.

To add to all the craziness—the confession, the calls from Father bragging about his infidelity, Grandmother keeping her up-to-date on what was happening within the family, and the church people bombarding her with gossip—Mother phoned to tell Jean she had learned of the affair (How could she not?), and Father had moved out of the house.

I cannot remember exactly how I felt at the prospect of returning home to find my father gone. For one thing, it sounded too good to be true. The thought of being free was a pretty heady experience for me, and I wondered if Mother felt anything like

I did. I wondered if my father would stay gone and hoped that he would. (Unfortunately, my grandmother called to say that he moved back home a few days later. Though short-lived, I did have my fairy tale daydream!)

It was, however, impossible for me to imagine a life without abuse, be it sexual, physical, or verbal. The patterns of behavior were so instilled within each of us in the family, that the idea of being on our own was unreal, even unnatural. None of us were ever taught how to be independent of one another. We had been part of the wickedness and subjugation for so long. I have learned, through therapy, that people tend to become so used to a particular type of behavior toward them, that they stay in bad relationships or dysfunctional families because they know nothing else, and to change is much more difficult than keeping the status quo. To regain control of one's soul and sanity is difficult and painful work. I know this first hand, and am reaffirmed each time I reread my manuscript and must deal with all the emotional garbage over and over again. One consolation is that I am able to become more detached as my story is edited, and it is only when I finish reading a chapter or passage that I allow myself to think about what I have just read. To read and reread one's own life story is awesome, to say the least. It is not that I attach any particular importance to my life as compared to others who have experienced similar abuse. I have the same emotions when I have read about the personal lives of the mistreated. Watching TV movies about abuse also lets these same emotions come forth. I am more and more relieved each time I read my own life history that it is history, and perhaps the sharing of The Secret will give others the strength and hope to do likewise allowing them to be in control of their own destinies.

Eventually the phone calls became an irritating nuisance. This differed from the disgust and pain of her father's disclosures. Jean found herself very tired of the entire mess. She took a very difficult, first step by seeking the input of a teacher who lived just below her dorm room.

A nagging voice in the rear of my consciousness, perhaps? Was this another brief confrontation by me, to me, that I desperately needed outside help? I think each of us who has been sexually abused as children, at some point in our horror, question the validity of our existence, and it is those moments we need to learn to recognize so that we may tell ourselves we do have value, and we are important, Then we will not hesitate to seek the help we need and must have in order to be truly free.

Jean could not disclose **The Secret**, so she skirted that issue and focused on her father's adultery and the annoying involvement of the church people. The teacher, who was unaware of deeper problems, told Jean she felt sorry for her but did not understand how Jean could remain in college while her family life was in such turmoil. Her school work would surely suffer.

Amazingly it did not and the end of the term showed a solid C+ average—not great, but not failing either. Jean was pleased with herself, and happy that she had been able to succeed while under the pressure of her father's crazy behavior.

Did she dare delude herself into planning for a future that included a college education, enabling her to leave Tuften and pursue a real life with a real career? Indeed, she dare not. Life, for her, was not to have ". . . and they lived happily ever after" ending.

In fact, her college career took an abrupt and disabling turn a few months later.

It did not seem so the summer of 19—when I met and married Charles. In retrospect, my marriage interfered with my education because I allowed it to happen, thinking I would be happier away from my family, in the security of a relationship my father could not touch or prohibit. This proved not so when Charles and I began having major problems—a direct result of my father's unrelenting prying and interference into my marriage relationship.

> Love is not in our choice,
> but in our fate.
>
> —Dryden

THE DECEIT OF HOPE

Jean's first semester of college had left her fearful of returning home, fearful that her life would take on the same sadness and despair. Getting away from home had not provided her, in most ways, the retreat she had hoped, but at least she had not had to deal with her father on a daily basis. The distress of Father's adultery was a long distance matter, making the problem seem unreal and, therefore, avoidable. Even so, Jean realized that she would have to go home again between fall and spring semester, and that meant being the focus (*nerve center*, as it were) of her father's verbal abuse.

Her fears, for once, were unfounded. Although there were none of the pleasantries of an affectionate family upon her arrival home for Christmas, there were no angry tirades either—no vicious words from the Patriarch. Quite the contrary. Jean, who had been suffering from an infected tooth, was encouraged to see a dentist for her problem.

This came as a surprise to me as any health-related problems were normally left untreated. Could it be that Father's straying from the bonds of matrimony had given Mother some control about which I was not aware? How would I ever discover the truth? It is becoming more and more obvious that some truths I will never learn, and that may be good. Then again, I may spend my life trying to discover that which will never be revealed. That could be time consuming and frustrating! Perhaps I have yet to reach that place of peace I eagerly seek—that unlittered highway leading to the safety of sanity.

In January, near the end of winter break and in a most likely place—church—Jean met her husband-to-be. She was ripe for a relationship that might rescue her from the certainty of loneliness, and she was aware that her internal, biological needs needed to be met. In the early 19—s, as other young women of her age and background, marriage and a family were part of her daydreams and hope for the future. It may be difficult to comprehend that a female person who has been sexually abused might want a husband. Jean not only was looking for an escape from her environment but she knew it was expected by society that she marry. Still, she was worried that her childhood experiences would influence her choice of men. What kind of man could someone such as she pick as a mate? Would she want a person different from what she was used to and make a wise decision? Or would she choose, from the dark recesses of her subconscious, a man like her father?

According to many studies I've read on the subject, we tend to pick mates based very much on the personalities left behind in the family—be they abusive families or not. Part of the human condition is not to see that which we do not wish to see, and so it was with me. I had no basis for comparison, outside the family, on which to judge the selection of a mate. I had no idea how to give and receive love except through the books I read and what I heard through the media. Story book romances were in vogue and that was what I strived for. Little did I realize the day I married, that although my husband never did present with the sexually abusive tactics of my father, he came close in other areas of his personality. But, I am getting ahead of myself. Enter Charles . . .

One Sunday morning in church Jean began talking to Jane, a young woman her own age whom she had seen several times before in the community. Their families had known each other for a long time, but were not on an intimately friendly basis. The girls' lively conversation that day led to an invitation to Jane's house the following Saturday where Jean was introduced to her new-found friend's brother, Charles. Charles asked Jean to go to church with him the next day and their attraction for each other proved to be the beginning of a life-long, emotionally garbage-laden commitment—far removed from reality as their hormones raged in January of 19—.

I was in love! To say I was surprised is a mild comment for what was taking place in my mind. Someone loved me, and I thought my good fortune a remarkable upturn of luck. After all, I was no beauty with my tall, awkwardly thin body, tipped with nondescript brown hair. I thought of myself as ugly, the product of a poor family of little community standing. I was not well-bred, pretty, or gracious. That a man could love me in spite of all my obvious faults was almost more than I could comprehend, yet it was what I had dreamed of in my most secret of romantic dreams.

The young couple's relationship gained momentum over the next few months. Whenever Jean was home from college, she spent the time with Charles and his sister. From January to May they wrote letters to each other or talked on the phone whenever it was possible. Charles was a quiet, pleasant man, noticeably thin, with red hair. Jean thought him very handsome, and in no way did he look like her father. He was the opposite of Jean's abusive father who was loud, aggressive, and visibly unhappy. She thought her happiness was Charles. She would finally live the fairy tale life. Again, it was fortunate for Jean's survival that she could not foresee the future.

In June, Charles asked Jean to marry him, both deciding on a September wedding. During the ensuing summer, the twosome spent most of their free time driving around in Charles's old blue and red car. They didn't have much money, but it did not matter. They enjoyed the simple pleasure of just being together.

Those were happy days for me. When I was apart from my life at home, the moments spent with Charles helped me to feel normal. I could not see anything at all wrong with the quiet young man who made me feel like a woman, very much protected and loved.

New problems beset Jean's family when she and Charles became engaged. Jean was not certain from which segment of the family this discontent with her engagement had emerged—whether Father was jealous and unwilling to let go, or Mother was jealous and wanted to negate Jean's happiness.

When I tried to show my mother the ring Charles had given me, she wouldn't even look at it. I don't think she ever looked at the ring. If she did, it was covertly when she thought I wasn't paying attention. She did lecture me for what seemed several hours that day, telling me how slow Charles was and how he would never be able to make a living for a family. The parting comment out of her mouth after the lecture was as painful to my emotional being as a bullet's penetration would have been to my brain. I can still hear her piercing scream in my mind, "I will not buy you a wedding gift because the marriage won't last a year!" I couldn't understand her reaction, but on looking back, I think Mother must have feared any of us children leaving home. It made her position that much more precarious. As long as we were available for Father's wrath and me for his sexual needs, she was afforded some security from the man's insanity. With six people living within the household, the abuse was not focused more on one person than another; it had a wicked balance. Without the four children, Mother would be Dad's only source of perversity—at least until grandchildren entered the picture.

Because they had no other recourse, Charles and Jean purchased their own wedding attire. Jean's father declared, predictably, that he would not pay for the reception. If he could not prevent the wedding, he could at least make it as unhappy an event as he had the power to do so.

How odd it felt then, and now, to be the preparer of one's own wedding without the aid of the parents, either financially or emotionally. It was as if the two of us were orphans. We were alone in our love for each other, no one with whom we could share our happiness—though we both had relatives in town! It was so bizarre, and I knew my family's stance was insensitive but I was in love with Charles. Nothing else mattered except that I escape into his home and out of mine.

When the people from the church Jean and Charles attended offered to provide the cake and punch for a small reception after the ceremony, the kindness was refused by Jean's parents without her consent. What would people think? It must not have occurred to them that people would be more prone to talk because Mother and Father neither paid for, nor allowed anyone else to pay for, a simple reception.

This hurt me deeply. No matter what the risk to their reputation, they were hell-bent on destroying my marriage before it began. I was convinced, at that time in my life, that I must have been a truly bad person to have them treat me as if I were totally unworthy. What should have been the most wonderful time of my life was nothing but another means to hurt and demean me. At no time did my mother consider my feelings. Fear was guiding her every action and if Dad did not want me to marry, neither did she. If Dad wanted me to be unhappy, so did she. She was not a mother to me. She was my nemesis. I couldn't put that label to her behavior, but I sensed that she hated me with passion. I certainly could not understand what was happening other than to blame it on my inadequacy as a human being. I knew Dad's refusal to pay any part of my wedding was not a matter of money. If it had been, he would have been only too pleased to tell me. I did think I should receive no less than the rest of the children would when they married. I knew my sister would get whatever she wanted; she always had. My brothers appeared to me as bad as I but I knew Mother and Dad would give them what they desired. My brothers were to prove me wrong in this regard, but then I had no idea of what was happening with the rest of my siblings. I was much too caught up in my own internal grief.

Although newlyweds have major adjustments during their first year of cohabitation, the changes taking place were more than Jean's understanding or belief. One month into the marriage things began to change—for the worse. Charles had a temper that Jean had never seen and his blow-ups frightened and puzzled her.

*I cannot remember precisely what my thoughts were, but I remember a sense of doom and a reaffirmation of my low opinion of myself. Was God continuing my punishment? How could this be happening to me? What made me so **bad** that I must endure over and over the verbal abuse that was destroying my self-esteem, my belief in my God, and causing me so much hatred and anger? It seemed as if my father possessed a demonic ability to transfer his insanity to my new husband.*

The young couple went to church every Sunday just as Jean's family had in the past. Just as her father had done, Charles used the scripture to try to control his new bride. Jean could hardly believe that she had married a man so much like her father.

Clearly, I know exactly what I thought when the realization hit me. I was not going to be like my mother whom I perceived as a weak person, and who used the same fear of God to keep control over her children. How was I to keep my behavior from imitating that of my mother's? A strength of will and strong determination to survive were all that I had as allies, and they were beginning to weaken and cause me severe emotional concern—metaphoric alarms were going off in my head and I was losing my sense of direction. I had not a clue as to how to stop the doubts and fears which were becoming my constant companions.

By the end of November, Jean was pregnant and morning sickness was more waking-hour sickness. In preparation for the birth of their first child, Jean and Charles earnestly discussed their ideas on raising children. Jean was shocked and afraid because her husband quoted scripture on raising children—again imitating her father's method of control.

I even contemplated terminating my marriage my fear was so tangible. The good times, however, outnumbered the bad—I thought. Also, what would I do if I divorced Charles? Go back to live with my parents, with a newborn in tow? Absolutely not! Some things are, indeed, worse than death. Besides, I was a good little church girl and it was ingrained in me that I must endure the role of the dutiful wife. Some thing was nagging at the back of my brain, though, and I think my inner self was trying to tell me it need not be so. I did not pay attention to my instincts for another 20+ years and the condition of my life continued its downhill, self-destructive ride into the garbage pit. I could not reach my safe house of security, yet. Somehow, deep within me, I knew it had to get better. I had no inkling that it would take so very long and waste so much time.

Charles and Jean's son, Buddy, was born in August. From the moment the baby arrived home from the hospital, Charles seemed uncomfortable. In the days that followed Charles's demeanor changed. He became visibly jealous and morose. Buddy, a very active baby, was a constant source of irritation to his father.

Charles and I argued almost every day about the baby and what I was doing wrong. My fear of his domination grew as memory after memory of physical abuse eroded my mental stability. I watched my baby like a hawk, determined to protect him and keep him from his own father—my husband. I didn't want Buddy to get beaten up as I had been and today it is hard for me to fathom the depth of my worry over my child, and my life.

Jean and Charles moved several times in the three years following their wedding. Jean hated moving as it was reminiscent of all the moves she and her siblings were forced to withstand during their growing-up years.

I could not put into words what it was about moving that caused me distress at that time. I now know that I must have equated it with the secrecy, the physical, mental and sexual abuse, and the total loss of my individuality. I could not express this to Charles because I did not know how, and I'm not too sure that he would have been receptive, then, to my emotional needs had I been able to get in touch with them myself.

By the next fall, there was another baby on the way.

Charles said he wanted another child but I wasn't quite as certain and told him this baby would be the last. Mental pictures of my mother being overpowered and constantly fatigued by the work and care of four youngsters was not appealing to me. I would be even more subjugated to the marriage, giving up more of the control I had over my time and sanity.

In March Kay was born. A less active child than her brother, the new baby was more content, quieter, and easier to care for. As a result, she did not cause her father as much concern. Jean's hopes for a more pleasant life within her small family did not seem quite as unrealistic.

The twenty years of reaching adulthood had been horrendous for Jean. She wanted the next twenty years to be different. The sexual abuse perpetrated by her father had come to an end. The verbal abuse would not stop for a long time and would be abetted by her husband.

Secretively, Father was playing a tremendous role in Charles's behavior since his immediate authority over Jean had changed. Charles, a susceptible and willing follower who believed the scriptures and their reference to women as subservient to their men, allowed his father-in-law into the day-by-day interaction of his home life. Charles did not know the maliciousness of the man who was his ruthless mentor, nor the extremes to which the man would go to regain control over Jean.

There was a laughing devil in his sneer,
that raided emotions both of rage and fear,
and where his frown of hatred darkly fell,
Hope, wither, fled, and mercy sighed farewell.

—Lavater

THE RESURRECTION
OF FATHER'S CONTROL

Subtly, like the cool, refreshing summer's breeze prior to a Florida hurricane, Father's influence over Charles blew ever so gently into the young family's life. From the eye of trust of the naive husband, outwardly to the ominous clouds of emotional destruction, to the menacing hate-words soon to pummel the delicate soil of sanity, the ill-fated storm grew powerful. Jean discovered that some of the advice given to her husband had originated from her father's mouth!

Was Charles even aware that he was under the control of this horrible creature a biological society labeled Father? I honestly do not think he was. I knew my father, but not even I suspected that he would penetrate our lives to the extent that he did. It is still very difficult for me to understand the full magnitude of the hold he had over all of us and how we fell willing prey to his need to devour us with his domination. This absolute power does help me to understand, however, how people can be robbed of their independence and individuality into the isolation of cult existence.

So it was that Father's advice on child-rearing passed to Charles, then to Jean, the unknowing participant in a new storm about to descend upon her and her family. Both she and Charles were strict, but Jean wanted no part of being as her parents had been. She wanted to let her children know that she believed in fairness and would keep a wary vigil over them when their need warranted that she do so—even if it meant that she defend them from her husband. She vehemently vowed to save them from the terror she had endured as a child, yet it was they who were the direct cause of the storm venting its wrath. Buddy, the first born, was active and sickly. He suffered from a milk allergy and asthma which periodically caused him to be fussy and difficult to pacify.

Who knows whether his predisposition to these particular maladies was caused by my own emotional trauma during his fetal development? Researchers and physicians provide their statistics, stating that such physical disorders are hereditary, but so are emotional dysfunctions. Does not one cause the exacerbation of the other? Of course, as a new mother I did not know any of this, but I am convinced now that we, who provided Buddy with his genetic code, provided both emotional and physical disabilities in conjunction. Buddy would not have had one—without the other!

As a result of Buddy's condition, Charles's patience wore thin, then disappeared. Jean had to spend time away from her husband to care for their child and this caused dissension within the marriage. The entire situation became a circular affair: Charles needed attention but was denied when Buddy needed attention; Buddy needed attention which caused Charles to become impatient; Charles demanded attention but the baby took precedence. On and on, day by day, Jean was caught in the middle, confused and angry with husband and child, but she repressed her feelings as she had been taught.

My happiness was slipping away into the black void of my childhood. I felt so internally desperate. I could not understand Charles's impatience and jealousy. Since Charles and I began counseling, I have learned that Charles felt denied in the care-taking of Buddy, thereby preventing him from bonding with his son. I do not believe this to be so because neither Charles nor I were aware of our own emotional needs and dysfunctions. Trying to go backwards with accusations is futile. Charles did not bond with

Buddy because of his own inadequacies. Not mine. Not Buddy's. This remains an area of some contention, but I feel confident we will resolve this as we have other disagreements about what took place in the early years of our marriage. Hope has become one of my most positive approaches to dealing with my past. If I could but allow patience to supersede, there, too, is hope . . .

During the difficulties with Buddy and Charles, Jean's father was in the background hiding—infecting Charles with the garbage with which he raised his children. In the background, a treacherous tempest (abuse) was brewing through an unwary, unsuspecting, young father and husband. Who but the most knowledgeable of human nature could have detected the early signs of this silent storm? Certainly not Charles. He was a naive boy-man being led ever so insidiously and quietly to his emotional, debris-cluttered, path of destruction. The fall-out, by natural course, was to encompass Jean and the children—Buddy in particular.

Thankfully I have overcome the blame I placed on Charles. He had no way of knowing what had taken place in my childhood because I had not yet taken him into my confidence. I had no way of knowing that my father was directing Charles's actions who truly, in his God-fearing manner, believed he was doing the right thing. Why should he doubt my father's advice? Hadn't the older man brought up four children? Hadn't he maintained a long-standing marriage? It took me a long time to admit that my father was a craftsman at the trade of deception. I should not have expected my husband to be any more perceptive than I.

Buddy, with each passing month, became more and more active, more and more of a bother to his father. By three months of age, the child was roaring about the house in a walker, exploring what his little hands could reach. He had his share of childhood illnesses, but they did not prevent him from being adventurous and active. At one year of age, he was running everywhere he went—walking took too long! He had a curious mind and an energetic body. Because of his development, Charles thought the little boy ready for discipline. He insisted

Buddy be spanked for every act of defiance or disobedience. Charles never considered that Buddy's age, lack of verbal skills, and an inability to reason, had not yet provided the child with the necessary maturity to understand what his father wanted or expected of him. Charles was raised with plenty of discipline and spankings and it did him no harm. His son was to be treated in a like manner. It had always been so, therefore, it was appropriate for his son.

Charles and I had many discussions about how Buddy should be treated. I deplored the idea of brutal spankings. I knew from my history that spankings made me hate, not respect or follow the rules of the household. Beatings led me to fear more of the same, not to respect my father or mother for pointing me in the right direction. It was while we were having one of our talks that I told Charles I wanted no more children if he persisted in his beliefs on the upbringing of our kids. I wanted no part of abuse. None! Somehow I knew that I had to stop the pattern which had been developed by my family—encouraged by my family. All the while Charles was following the advice of my father without my knowledge, a tiny bit of doubt and suspicion was beginning to build as to where Charles's attitudes were coming from because of the similarity to my father's.

My mother, however, was not without her sick part in Buddy's regard. Although she was not abusive in any way to my child, she continued her verbal abuse of me as time after time she would bring clothes for the baby, or loan us money for his medicine. The gifts were not freebies. They had a high price for me. Each one brought a lecture about Charles's sorry state as a provider, with an "I told you so" thrown in as a measure to force me into humiliation and submission in her presence. It worked. She knew it would and I fell into her trap again and again. I was always left with a feeling of inadequacy, that Buddy would not have to "do without" if I were a better person, and that Mother would not punish me if I were not so bad. Charles unwittingly abetted Mother's behavior—insult to injury—when it came to money. He had a steady job but we still struggled from payday to payday.

Some of our most energetic, angry discussions (fights) concerned money. There was never enough to go around and I felt it was my fault even though I was not the provider. If I were a better person, Charles would have a better job. If I were a better person, I would know how to handle the paltriest of pay checks. Even after three years of counseling and group involvement, I find myself feeling these same inadequacies and wonder if I shall ever be able to get rid of the emotional beatings I continue to exact on myself when I'm feeling down or depressed. This does not happen with a regular occurrence anymore, and seems to be more prevalent in specific areas of my life, but it does happen and I still sense that I am not quite adequate.

Into an already strained existence arrived the baby girl—a docile child, easily pleased. Charles and Jean were no longer novice parents, and Kay's easy going nature may have reflected this fact. The tension of handling a small person no longer existed, creating a calming effect on the newborn. This, in turn, gave Charles more confidence with his baby daughter than he had with his son. She was less squirmy and wiggly, more open to her father's closeness.

Kay, like Buddy, did present with many health problems. Apparently her parents, though more experienced with babies, genetically passed along an inherent emotional instability. Kay was simply quieter about whatever anxiety went on in her little mind. Time would tell that the emotional unhappiness of the mother would transfer itself to the daughter in a most unusual way.

Within a few weeks of Kay's birth, Jean noticed the baby's hands were shaking. At first she thought it a normal, involuntary response to stimuli. When the condition persisted, it was obvious something was definitely wrong.

It was eight years later that I took Kay to a physician for her tremors. I can't remember why it took me so long to recognize that my daughter's condition would not go away by itself. I can't even remember if I was afraid of what a physician would say, or if money was the reason. Since I did take my daughter to an eye doctor when she was nine months old, I find this last statement indigestible. Some of what happened in my past is lost entirely. Generally that happens when the memory is terribly distressing to me or if I suffer from massive guilt.

Jean's mother, who doted on Kay, was the first to make a comment about the child's eyes. They did not look normal in a close-up snapshot which had been taken of the baby a few weeks before. Jean immediately made an appointment with the eye doctor, but the condition was not fixed, nor would it be for another 14 years.

Hand tremors and eye problems aside, Kay had the usual childhood illnesses, along with some persistent conditions affecting her throat and lungs. Her developmental skills were slow in forthcoming, such as walking and talking. Still, Kay was an easy child; she didn't cry much and got along with her daddy who thought of her as his pride and joy. The magnitude of Kay's health problems had only touched the surface of what was to come in the future and what would cause the emotional abyss between Jean and her mother to widen.

I really thought my mother had caused me as much grief and sadness possible to inflict on one individual. I expected my father to continue his verbal abuse of me, but I thought my mother would treat me differently once I was a married woman—like an adult or a woman friend. How wrong I was! While walking through a store on a shopping trip with Mother, I asked her if she remembered what day it was. When she didn't answer, I informed her it was my 21st birthday. She looked at me as if she didn't know who I was, then turned toward a counter, picked up a bottle of hand lotion, passed it to me and said, "Here. This is for your birthday." Unbelievable? Painful? I was removed from pain and disbelief. I was stunned. Her actions absolutely, undeniably, verified that I was something other than human in my mother's eyes. My days were an endless array of new sorrows. I felt myself drowning in depression when I realized that both Mother and Dad were determined to keep me under their sick, emotional umbrella. Why? If I was so unimportant, why did they spend so much time trying to make me miserable? That question plagued me then; it does so today.

Jean tried very hard to do what was best for her two children. At the same time her parents interfered in her marriage and in how the kids were being raised. Jean did not have the courage to tell them to butt out—to leave Charles and her alone to create their own lives within their own family unit. Charles seemed so compliant and obviously in total agreement with Jean's father. Perplexed and confused most of the time, Jean's ability to cope with her life situation was at risk. She cringed whenever Father was near her children, that he might sexually abuse them as he had done her. She never felt at peace, even when she had settled the kids down for the night and she and Charles fell into bed with total exhaustion. Every waking hour of every day, Jean worried and fretted. She knew, deep down within her soul, that Father was aware of her distress and was laughing secretly. Jean felt he knew she was attached to him emotionally in a sick and sad way, and it can be presumed that his delight was evil and consuming because he was not normal. He was a madman who had fooled the outside world. He was a madman who would never once spend a night in jail for the rape of his child's body and mind. He had regained control of his oldest child and he, in his madness, should have been content.

He was not. Nor would he be until he had destroyed Jean and her husband and children. He would not be content until he defiled everything he had the power to defile. Power was never complete for him unless the destruction was complete. Even his own . . .

A malady
Preys on my heart, that medicine cannot reach
Invisible and cureless.

—Maturin

INFIRMITIES OF MIND, BODY AND SOUL

A Family's Legacy

Jean evolved agonizingly through her 20's, from the fearful daughter to an apprehensive and disappointed housewife. Even her role as a parent was frustrating and frightening, with Buddy's asthma and Kay's undiagnosed afflictions. Jean's daily existence was as if it were framed in depression which surrounded a canvas of voiceless desperation. More and more, in her mind, she questioned her sanity, trying—with futility—to confront her unhappiness in order to ease her emotional burden. She was sick inside, and though she thought the primary cause rested with her father and 20 years of physical and emotional abuse, she did not know how to bring herself up and out of the despair which had overtaken her very soul.

At that time in my life I still had not consciously focused any anger and hate toward my mother. Though I felt she did not defend me, nor comfort me in times of emotional need, I still blamed my father for most of my psychological difficulties. I wanted desperately to hang onto that one thread of hope that mother, when she reached her bottom, would take me into her arms and heart and nurture us both to good mental health. I still cannot let go of that hope even as the thread becomes more worn and fragile as time passes and mother and I have not resolved anything.

As Jean's father became fully embroiled in his determination to undermine Jean and her family, his own physical and emotional decline was manifesting as visible entities. Apparently he did not (or could not) see his medical problems as having any correlation to his own mental illness. (One has only to research some of the medical literature to learn that the two can have a very adverse relationship.) As his physical and mental condition worsened, so did that of Jean's mother, as though what Father had was communicable—as indeed it had seemed so throughout their marriage.

Was this a just punishment for Dad's transgressions against nature, his God, and the very laws created to protect people from abuse, especially children? Did Dad's evil deeds become etched into the very fabric of his being, eventually causing a slow, pervasive decay from his inner self to the outside where people could witness the degradation of his years of habitual abuse, exacted upon those he professed to love? Did this even show upon his face? What of Mother who had aided and abetted in much of the abuse? Was the bitterness I saw upon her face visible to others? Was this, too, a sign of sickness? Now I know that it was. At the time, I could only guess.

Jean began to take note of her father's physical and mental deterioration. For a man in his 40's, he presented a picture of a much older man whose illness was speeding up the aging process. He began to drink more often and Jean rarely saw him at home without a beer in his hand. If they all went out to dinner, he always had a cocktail or a glass of wine.

This in itself did not indicate that Dad was an alcoholic. His behavior, however, belied the, "I can take a drink now and then," rationalization, or "I'm a man, I can handle my liquor." He became even surlier and meaner than I could remember from my childhood. In fact, it has only been recently that I was aware that he drank when I was growing up; and if it hadn't been for the home movies which were processed into VHS tapes after Dad's death, and shown to me, I would still question that fact. I was amazed when those old home movies revealed my father was rarely without a beer in his hand. He was drinking while he sat, when he was working around the house or yard, while he stood, when the camera caught him by surprise. Mother, whose obvious role it had always been to protect the good family name, could possibly have been a secret service agent for all that I knew about Dad's drinking. I felt exonerated for the part I played in trying to get mother to face his alcohol problem when I was in my twenties. The excuses she had made for Dad, saying that it was impossible for a man who went to work every day and never drank in the morning, to be an alcoholic, had no validity anymore. I know for certain that Mother conveniently forgot the time she had caught Dad urinating in one corner of their bedroom, or the time Dad rammed his arm through the bedroom window. I remember feeling put down because of my observations. How dared I question her about Dad's indiscretions? What would people think if I let it out that Dad drank too much? God forbid the world should know the truth!

Father's ill-use of time, as he plundered the psyches of his children well into their adulthood, was turning against him. Time became his opponent—a harbinger of mental, as well as physical, atrophy.

A fall from a truck at his place of work caused a severe injury to Father's ankle. His doctor, not knowing the history of alcohol abuse, prescribed codeine for pain, on which Father soon became dependent. When his physician denied him the prescriptive source of codeine, Father found another.

My dad's cousin's wife was also taking codeine at the time of Dad's injury. I discovered that she would share some of her prescription with Dad, taking his word for it that he needed it for pain and he couldn't get it. I was sure that this woman meant no harm, but she was unaware of Dad's drug dependency. I decided to intervene by telling her that Dad was not only addicted to the codeine, but that he took the pills in conjunction with hard liquor. I impressed upon her that if he should die because of this combination of drugs, she would be partly responsible. She immediately stopped providing the codeine and every once in a while, after that conversation, Dad would comment: "What ever happened to my cousin's wife? She never brings me my pills anymore." His addiction was so great that this lady's pills had become his and he expected her to be a constant source of his needs!

Also, along with the alcohol abuse and mental illness, Father was presenting with other medical maladies. He noticed that a lump had formed on the scar from an appendectomy. Although he never considered taking one of his children or wife to the doctor (because of the expense), he tended to his own needs with no thought to cost. Thus it was that he took himself to a physician when the lump was discovered, thinking that he had a possible hernia. Surgery revealed that the lump was cancerous. One week after being released from the hospital, Father was readmitted and surgery was performed to remove a testicular cancer.

Strangely enough, my father and his father (my grandfather) each had one testicle that had not descended during the growth process within a short time after birth—a process that occurs in normal male development. With what I have learned through my own questioning, through counseling, and reaching my own conclusions, that may explain some of Dad's concerns with regard to his own masculinity. His father was abusive and suffered similar health problems, which were definitely male-oriented. Another male family member, whose record for broken marriages may one day surpass the current statistics in Ripley's Believe It Or Not for the number of times being married, also suffers from low male self-esteem. Could they all have shared a common hang-up about what comprises a male person? I can look upon these questions as a topic I might like to research. I long to know why people behave the way they do, particularly those who worked so hard to inhibit my emotional growth. I was beginning to realize, way back in the first ten years of my marriage, that Mother's physical problems were also very much connected to being married to my dad and the denigration she allowed herself to endure. I still have trouble understanding why my mother tolerated our abuse, but at least I can see that her youth had been stolen from her. When I was 24 and my mother 40, she seemed old, beaten down, and sickened by life's cruelties.

Jean's mother was becoming more and more emotionally distraught and soon her mental condition brought with it a myriad of physical disabilities. She looked frail and sickly, complaining of this or that ailment, not easily able to verbalize the source of her discomfort. That her physical pain was real to her was evidenced by her incapacity to deal with the reality, and the fact that no physician could explain why her body was behaving as it did when she was convinced something was wrong. She once fell in the street as she was walking, having lost all conscious control and strength of movement, as if she had been inflated, like a balloon, and someone had stuck a pin in her outer structure. She was taken by ambulance to the hospital where she was examined thoroughly, yet the doctors could find nothing physiologically wrong. Mother also suffered anxiety attacks in which her throat would actually close to the passage of food or air. She became inexplicably frightened of the outside world and preferred the safety of her home. There was a terrifying moment at the beauty shop—a place she frequented—when a horrible fear overcame her. She was certain that if she walked outside she would die.

My mother explained to me that she thought her anxiety was caused by allergies—perhaps subconsciously suggesting that the proper medicine might be all that she needed. I now know there is a name for her condition: agoraphobia.

As Mother's anxiety grew, so did her physical ailments. She developed stomach distress so severe she could not lie flat in bed to sleep at night. Acid backed up into her esophagus, her throat and her mouth. The pain was displayed on her face as her pale pallor implied, and vomiting was not unusual.

She could not keep the pain a secret had she tried. It was too observable by those around her. She found some relief if she raised her head during sleep time, but the pain persisted as the inner turmoil she must have been experiencing persisted.

Depression became a common word to Jean's mother as she verbalized her feelings to the daughter who silently screamed for love and acceptance. "I feel so low and unhappy," Mother would say. "I've felt like this for weeks and I don't care if I live. I have nothing to live for."

My own needs, however, far outweighed those of my mother. My own sickness took precedence in my mind. Why couldn't she see how hurt I was? Was I expected to give her the kindness she seemed to be seeking when she had never provided the same for me? I wonder if I could have felt, or did feel, compassion or empathy toward my mother's sadness and pain. Since my dad's death, Mother gives out bits and pieces of her feelings and maybe, just maybe, she is trying to come to grips with the part she played in the dysfunctional family she helped create. I am not witness to this behavior, but my daughter has been. There was a time when Mother never watched the talk shows whenever they dealt with sexual, physical, or emotional abuse. She does now, and Kay has said Mother will periodically stare off into space, as if relating to or remembering something from her past.

There is an old saying that begins: "The sins of the father . . ." Whatever else follows is much too passive for what Jean's father and mother caused to happen, then insisted did not happen, while the children were growing into young adults. They passed to their child Jean the sins, the sadness, the perversity, the sickness. Their legacy was boundless in the physical destruction that took place then. Within the family, which no longer remotely thought of itself as a unit as far as Jean knew, maladies of all kinds prevailed as she tried to secure her own sanity and health, isolated in self-made, or inherited, despair.

Jean, with some unknown strength, entered into her thirties demanding answers within herself, not wanting the legacy that was hers. To whom and where could she turn? How could she deny the inheritance of aberrant behavior and sick emotions! One day she would find her truth and her peace, but for the time being, her search would deadlock.

Talk not of comfort,
Tis for lighter ills;
I will indulge my sorrows,
and give way to all the pangs of despair.

—Addison

Road Blocks, Dead Ends, and Locked Doors

Jean's marriage and subsequent parenthood was reminding her more and more of her life as a child. She and Charles lived in six different houses in the first three years of their marriage, never quite settling down in a place they could call their own. They argued about the children frequently, because Charles was behaving like her father in many of his actions. He used scripture from the Bible to try to control his wife, just as Jean's father had done.

I thought I was stuck in a time warp where every time I tried to go forward an action or interaction would push me back and I would relive my childhood terror over and over. The mind control Charles tried to exert was so much like that of my dad's, I felt like the push-me pull-me in the Dr. Doolittle story: scripture to repress me, having babies to appease me, father to push me, mother to pull me. Dear God, it was crazy and I knew it, but I could not even see an open window or doorway through which I could make my escape into sanity.

Jean was beginning to reach a breaking point. The unsettling moves were causing deep stress. Health problems of the children strained the young couple's budget and patience, and the atmosphere around Jean choked her ability to reach out for some kind of help. When Jean was 26, her father decided to move to a new home and sell his house to one of his adult children. As could be expected, he offered the house to Jean's siblings first. Only after they declined, did he ask Jean and Charles if they would like to buy the house and make it their permanent home.

Jean knew that she had been last choice again, but she saw the offer as an escape from the moving syndrome. To Jean, buying the house from her father-persecutor did not seem to be a wise decision, but it was at a price she and Charles could afford. She did not even consider what the consequences down the years might be, nor how the purchase would connect her even deeper to the family's evil legacy, for it would be in this house that Mother finally admitted something definitely was wrong with Father.

The first time Mother acknowledged the abuse, I cried for hours. Then I promised myself that I could not let the tears flow one more time; it hurt too much. I kept my promise for ten years, locking the tears safely away. No one could or would ever see me cry again. I felt I had reached a dead end in my life—a closed chapter providing a dam behind which all the litter on my roadway to maturity was stored. What I did not realize was that if the dam's basic structure was continuously deluged with emotional garbage, its walls would crumble, flooding my life's road with insurmountable obstructions.

In May of 19—, Jean turned 30 years old, her youth and her past slipping away into a labyrinth of confused perceptions and unresolved grief as new pain was added and stored in her mind. The control of her parents was paramount, interfering with her new family. Her siblings, seizing the unspoken rules of destructive conduct from her parents, perpetrated the emotional abuse of Jean and her husband. Meanness crept into the social interactions between Jean, Charles, and Jean's family. The family gave Charles joke gifts for birthdays and Christmas, never caring that the jokes were cold and unkind.

The truth be known, I believe the joke gifts were given as a put down. Like children on the playground who torment their weaker peers and who seek only to be boss, my biological family had to prove time after time their ability to control those symbolic children on the playground. Though generally not fully aware of the unkindness of their actions, children are simply testing their abilities to retain their own space. My family, on the other hand, knew full well the extent of the agony they could execute on the already thrashed nucleus of my soul. Oh, they were experts in cold-blooded cruelty!

Jean couldn't understand the unkind acts perpetrated on her husband Charles who had never been unkind to his in-laws. He was innocently unaware of the fun being made of him. He trusted that Jean's family liked and accepted him, but Mother was constantly telling Jean that Charles was unworthy, and Father delighted in feeding damaging information to Charles regarding the care of his children.

I should have realized sooner that the family would not have treated Charles any differently than they treated me. I was, after all, a bad person. Why else did I deserve the abuse I received? Charles and I were left out of family parties. We were judged and condemned without democracy, and I constantly felt abandoned. One would think it would have been obvious to me that my family was sick, and I was better off without them, but I was so unhappy and so in need of acceptance that I constantly overlooked the awful truth. I would never have a normal loving family. Had I faced that truth, however, I may not have survived at all but given in to my depression and done away with myself after all. I sincerely believed I was the cause of how others perceived and treated me. I was no longer in God's care for if I had been, I would have been taken care of in a kinder way. I was so bad. If there was one ability I had during these painful years, it was the ability to emotionally beat the hell out of myself—as do many of us who have survived abuse. We really do tend to place blame with ourselves, not our abusers.

When Jean and Charles's daughter was seven years old, her physical and intellectual disabilities couldn't be ignored. She had tremors in her hands and lack of muscle control in her eyes. When she was a toddler she had been slower than other children in learning to walk and talk. Also, she had spent two years in mainstream classes before she was officially diagnosed as having a learning disability and was placed in a class for handicapped children. Mother could not accept that her granddaughter was less than normal and was livid with Jean's and Charles's decision to place Kay where she would receive the best education with her specific limitations. Mother would insist many times over that Kay was normal, that there was nothing wrong with her.

My friend and co-author suggested to me a long time ago that my mother could not accept Kay's diagnosis because she considered it an affront against the normalcy of the family, as if she (Mother) were defensive. What would people say if they knew her granddaughter was less than perfect? That would confirm that Mother was less than perfect and she couldn't allow the outsiders of the world know this. When Kay went to Mother's house she tried to teach her how to read and invariably said, "See? There's nothing wrong with my granddaughter." Instinctively I knew what was best for my daughter and Mother's bad track record for making choices was so poor in her own life, I did not trust her to make the right choices for my daughter.

When Kay was placed in a class for students with special needs, Jean decided to volunteer at the school where her daughter attended. She had never worked outside her church or her home. To put herself in a new setting was unusual and difficult. The decision was a formidable one, but Jean was determined to provide the emotional support she had never received, to be of value and assistance to her daughter. If that meant placing herself in the uncomfortable position with people she didn't know, she would somehow overcome her discomfort.

I never did conquer my feelings of inadequacy during the time I worked at Kay's school. I felt so separate from others, so different that I did not relate well. At least two women tried to get through my thorny exterior, but the walls I had involuntarily created around myself did not allow them into my inner sanctum.

I didn't have a clue as to why I was the way I was, and I could not understand why people reacted toward me the way they did. I felt very much like an outcast, never quite able to form attachments or friendships with the other women who worked as volunteers at the school. It never occurred to me that my demeanor may have frightened others away, that people could sense my own discomfort and, in turn, this caused them to keep their distance. There were times when I wanted to scream at those who seemed to shun me, "What's going on? What's wrong with me?" I never did because it would have created too much attention to be focused on me, and I was used to hiding. Even though I felt very deeply that I was unloved because of some fault of my own, I did not want this reaffirmed by outsiders. Can it be that I created some of my own confusion due to all the mixed messages I had received during my youth? Of course, many people who are from dysfunctional families have received a distorted sense of what's right and what's wrong—with them.

In spite of the inner and outer turmoil in Jean's life, the volunteer work gave her a sense of accomplishment and worth. Kay, who was seven, enjoyed her mother at school. When her parents were separated during the time Charles was at work, and away from the house, Kay did not have to listen to them fight.

The kids knew their parents argued about discipline all the time. What Jean did not realize was she did to her children what she vowed she would not do, arguing in front of them. Jean felt unsafe when her parents got into screaming fights. Her children must have felt the same way.

There were times during the first ten years that the family became a true family, sharing and going places together as a unit. Outings to the beach were especially fun and rewarding, as were the fishing trips where the family camped out and enjoyed nature. Those times were very dear to Jean because they were able to have fun without the stress of everyday problems and she was able to forget about her internal pain for awhile.

Many of the problems Jean had in her marriage were directly related to the sexual abuse she received as a child, though her memory of specific events was lost. Certain behavior on Charles's part triggered strange and inexplicable behavior in response. He innocently directed Jean to put more water in the bath tub and Jean flew into a rage, "Don't tell me what to do! You aren't my daddy!"

Neither of us understood what was causing me to react the way I did. For Charles it must have been a total puzzle, but for me it was frightening and left me drained of stable emotion. I finally went to my pastor and told him about the problems in my marriage. It was not an easy decision for me to expose my feelings, but I knew I had to do something. To take the first step forward to a normal life I explained to my pastor that I had been sexually molested by my father, and his response was almost as destructive as the verbal abuse of my father. I was told by the man who professed to be a man of God that the world had worse problems, that I should let mine go and it would be all right. But it was not all right! My home situation along with the mental stress became much worse. Charles and I ended up in shouting matches which left me feeling like no one understood and even worse, no one cared. Several years after my thwarted session with the first pastor, a new pastor told me the same thing. I was trying to get some help and was crushed to learn he did not know how to help me either. I realized that help would not come from the church. I had been taught that if I was a true Christian, help would always come through prayer and counseling through the church. If a person had to go outside the church then something must be wrong with the person: James 1:6: "But let him ask in faith with no doubting."

Somehow I thought God would swoop down and solve all these problems of mine because I asked. When it did not happen, I was sure that I must be at fault. After all, the Bible said, "Ask and you will receive, seek and you will find." I felt like a small child. The church people treated me as if I were stupid.

Jean had one friend, Maggie, who knew about the terrible sexual abuse she has suffered. This friend advised Jean that she should just love her father, that was what she had done with her stepfather who had sexually abused her. Jean resented the advice because she felt she did not love her parents, that she had tried very hard to get them to love her and accept her as the person she thought she was. Her friend's advice was not acceptable and when Jean tried to explain this, she sensed that Maggie was drained by her emotional state.

Sometime prior to this particular incident I finally broke down and told Maggie about my childhood. It was really the first time I had enough courage to talk about the abuse to anyone. I remember sitting in a car talking to my friend. I was objecting to the way my parents were treating me. Maggie told me that I had no business complaining so much. I had not been raped as she had been when she was a little girl. I screamed at her, "Oh, yes I was!" I didn't eat or sleep for four days. My husband wanted to know what was going on, so he became the second person with whom I shared my horror—the Secret. It was many years later before I broached the subject again, except I did advise my children to beware of evil in grandfather's clothing. Though I didn't exactly make it sound so harsh, that was what I thought.

Jean spent many hours of worry regarding her children and the person who was their biological grandfather. She feared every waking moment that her father would molest Buddy or Kay and cringed whenever the children were in the company of her father. She knew it was her job to protect them from what had happened to her. To provide a mother's shield against the terrors of a sick family, her instincts were sharp and one wonders where and how she could overcome the weakness of her own mother when that was all she had been taught. "Having a mother did not mean one was safe" (Forward 158). It may mean quite the opposite, as it had in Jean's own family.

She warned the children in the best way she knew how, without causing undue fear in their young minds. She didn't want them to hate their grandfather (religious convictions and the need for love die hard), just understand that he was not to be trusted, particularly in a situation where they found themselves alone with him. She had to protect her children from a lifetime of pain at any cost to her own psychological equilibrium.

The end of Jean's first decade of marriage was anything but happy. Fun or the idea of having fun was slowly ebbing away into the voluminous garbage pit of problems besetting the young couple. Charles had a job, but didn't make much money. Bills were piling up and the stress of that fact was overpowering. Jean and Charles fought all the time. Jean was still unaware of her father' interference and ongoing advice to Charles regarding the rearing of the children and the treatment of his wife.

I don't think Charles knew he was being manipulated by my father, but I finally had an inkling because of one incident. I remember quite clearly that I had been cleaning house one morning and Charles came and asked why I hadn't dusted under the bed. I said, "I know where that came from." Charles admitted that my father told him to make sure I swept under the bed.

Other things were not as easy. I learned, after much counseling (and disbelief, at first), that because of the patriarchal domination as I was growing up—and being used to harsh conduct—I was psychologically drawn to a man who was very much the same as my father. When I was in my early 30s though, I would have denied this truth, even when Charles employed the Scripture to gain control over me. Funny, it almost worked.

Jean had gone to church all her life, and it seemed that the ways of the church were to obey one's parents regardless of the brutality of those parents, and obey one's husband and the brutality of that husband. Jean's parents told her this many times, and she believed it as a youngster. It didn't make sense, but Jean knew she had better comply without question. To do otherwise would have been considered an act of defiance against God. In her father's eyes, to dispute his authority was to subject oneself to violent punishment.

This twisted thinking stayed with me until my late 20s when I questioned how anyone could use the Scripture as a tool to control, committing violent acts against children or controlling women as if they were second class citizens. When three weeks into our marriage my husband displayed the same attitudes and beliefs as my father, I was in a state of disbelief. Charles also told me he was the boss and what he said was the ruling force of the family. In my state of shock I responded that I wanted a husband, not another father to rule over me with an iron fist. Charles reiterated that he was the man and being in control was his God given right. Our church taught this same superior attitude, and I hated hearing it because I knew it was wrong. As I look back down that painful road, part of what I received I felt I asked for. I played dumb out of fear. I was afraid of so many things. As a result, Charles did take care of paying the bills, going with me when I purchased the groceries, and running errands. I prayed that he didn't know how afraid I was of him and his forced dominance.

Jean's hope for a peaceful existence was rapidly waning as each new problem compounded the old, creating more and more roadblocks in the pathway to emotional safety. She felt lost and alone up in her head as she tried to deal with a husband who behaved like her father. The children's physical difficulties worried her. Her mother's attitude and indifference pained her deeply, yet she kept trying to receive approval.

Her siblings treated her as if she were a stranger with a grotesque plague. She was never included in their activities. Rather than talk to each other as adult, mature people, they fought when they were together. Other people told Jean that her siblings said bad things about her, and Jean believed they were telling the truth. Being rejected by her brothers and sister was no different from being rejected by her parents. It hurt terribly.

Jean was almost 40 years old and nothing, absolutely nothing, had changed. She was still a victim hiding from the world, detesting her reality. Her life was stuck in an emotional limbo, neither going forward or backward. Her thoughts were focused on self-destruction and hate and anger toward her family. She sensed that if she did not receive help soon she would be lost to depression and despair until the day of her death.

> The best sort of revenge
> is not to be like him who did the injury.
>
> —Antoninus

THE END AND . . .
THE BEGINNING

By the time Jean was 40 years old she had two teenage children and a husband she loved, but with whom she did not get along. She spent almost all her waking hours with her own family or at church. Wherever she went, Mother was there. Sometimes she felt sorry for her mother and much of the time her Mother's presence allowed Jean to feel an essential part of her mother's life. She finally felt important to this woman who gave her birth, that she was good for something, if only to provide Mother with company so that she would not feel or be alone, or for transportation when the need arose. In the back of her mind Jean may have felt used, but at least she was getting the attention she desperately needed and wanted. The trade-off seemed worthwhile.

Father was becoming more and more sullen. He rarely went out of the house except to go to work. He never attended the graduations of his grandchildren and only went to one of their weddings. He went to work, came home and sat with a beer in one hand and a long, smelly, lighted cigar in the other. Periodically he would go to the store if he ran out of alcohol or smokes. The television was his only source of company, and he avoided interacting with anyone. He wouldn't take his wife anywhere. When Mother had headaches so severe she could not see, he wouldn't take her to the doctor. Her life and her pain were as insignificant to him as were his children's lives and pain. He was an exploiter of souls, cared for no one, and his wife was simply another non person to him. Even if she became ill, he expected her to tend to his selfish wants and be a willing recipient of his admonitions.

Father was 61 years old and behaving as if he were 81. He displayed absolutely no energy except in vitriolic words spoken to anyone who spoke to him first. Age was not mellowing this man who had the mindset of a very disturbed, sick individual who grew, internally, more so with each passing day. He was spent on his own hate and need to dominate every member of his family.

It must be remembered that Father was not the solitary tyrant of what he considered his domain. Mother was no angel. She provided her own form of emotional abuse and control over her oldest daughter. When Jean's husband would pick up Mother to go to the doctor, or wherever she needed to go, she seemed to delight in starting a fight between her daughter and son-in-law. She laughed shrilly with absolute pleasure.

If Jean introduced a new friend, her mother turned sour and withdrew just as she did when Jean was a child. Jean often felt like a child needing her mother's approval still. The only way to get along with Mother was to do what she wanted, agree with whatever she said, and most of all, Jean must not bring another friend into her life.

Jean and Charles found a physician who could fix Kay's eyes. This involved a monthly trip to San Francisco. Mother accompanied the couple on every trip (except for the first surgery), going by train. It was Kay's second surgery that Charles told Jean he was tired of Mother chaperoning them on every trip and the subsequent hassles with her behavior and acerbic attitude. He was firm in his decision and told Jean, "Don't ask her to go with us until you ask me first." This was not easy as Jean spoke to her mother every day on the phone. *It is not difficult to see—now—the part I played in my own emotional destruction. I felt obligated to tell mother what*

I was doing, where I was going, and when I would be home. I didn't wish to annoy her in any way, fearing she would find fault with my behavior. She was never one to hold back her displeasure with me, and I couldn't deal with any more rejection. She knew this and used this to keep me in line. Yet, in this one instance, and maybe for the first time, I abetted my husband's words and Mother went with us less and less. I hoped—no, prayed—that she would make a life for herself, without being such an active part of ours. She didn't. She transferred her needs to her other daughter and to her daughter-in-law with whom she did get along. But, my sister and sister-in-law felt sorry for Mother, as I did, and we continued to try and please her as we had as children, hoping that we would be reciprocated with some emotional support, with unconditional love. We should have known that it was useless to expect emotional support as a fair exchange for being attentive.

Each passing day seemed to bring with it additional emotional pain. Father spent his time up in his head, totally alienated from reality. Mother spent most of her days trying to control the female members of the family with guilt and sorrow. Charles was still trying to dominate his wife. Jean was trying desperately to understand why her entire life had been so miserable. Her state of mind was in a delicate balance between wanting what she considered a normal life and self-destruction.

If someone had told Jean she was going to suffer more pain in her immediate future than she had ever before imagined, she would have denied the possibility. Nothing could ever compare to the abuse she had suffered as a child.

The most profound event that was considered the end of family unity and sanity arrived quietly and unexpectedly one day in the spring of 19—, in the shape of a uniformed officer and a social worker. Jean was sitting in her living room, Charles was at work, and their children were at school.

Jean heard a knock at her front door and wondered who was coming to visit. She was not expecting anyone. As she opened the door, a man in a sheriff's uniform was standing with a woman Jean recognized from her high school days. The sheriff's officer introduced himself, displaying his badge. The woman did likewise, displaying a badge from Social Services.

"Is there a problem? Jean asked.

The officer responded, "No. We would just like to talk to you."

An uneasy feeling began to creep up her spine, but in no way did she have a clue of the emotional bomb to be dropped in her living room that day. She invited the couple into the house.

With great calm the social worker said, "We know your father sexually abused you. Furthermore, we think he abused other children. We want to prove it."

Just like that Jean's world came crumbling down around her. She felt like a guilty defendant on the witness stand as the sheriff asked for a detailed account of what her father had done. For the next two hours Jean cried so hard it was difficult to talk. She was isolated from the emotional support of anyone who loved or cared about her. She felt outside herself as she related a past she wished was not hers.

Jean told the two strangers things she had never exposed to anyone. She was devastated within as she felt the dam hiding her past burst, releasing a flood of emotion.

As the two people left her home, after turning her life upside down, the Social Worker patted her gently on top of the head and said, "Please consider some counseling."

Jean silently pleaded, "Dear God, what is happening to my life? How did they know?"

Ten years after this incident I learned who had disarmed the family defenses. Wife number five of my oldest brother exposed the family history to the outside world. The day the sheriff and social worker came to my home, however, was the day I was blamed for it all. Mother said that if I had refused to talk to the sheriff no one outside the family would have been any the wiser. She was determined to blame me because I had always been the perfect scapegoat.

When Jean's daughter Kay arrived home from school that fateful day, she informed Jean what the sheriff had said to her at school, that he asked if she had been sexually abused by her grandfather. Neither of Jean's children was surprised at the revelation of the social worker. Jean had talked to Buddy and Kay through their growing up years about the sickness of their grandfather. And, because of Jean's protection of her children, Kay was able to honestly tell the sheriff that her grandfather had not molested her in any way.

Jean was informed that the sheriff's officer talked to her nieces and nephews, but that her brothers and sister refused to speak to him. So much emotional garbage was bombarding Jean's senses: the sexual abuse she had suffered; the painful trauma of physical abuse; and the spiritual abyss caused by the hate and despair she felt as a child. She was in a state of shock, crying and wondering what had happened and why.

Shortly after Kay's arrival home, Jean's mother called and confronted her with the question, "Did your father sexually abuse you?" "Yes, he did," Jean answered fearfully. Her thoughts screamed at her. All hell is going to break loose. She started to cry again. Mother did not ask what Father had done, so Jean concluded that her mother had known all the facts prior to the arrival of the sheriff at the door. Mother's confrontation was to cover up her own guilt in the perpetration of the abuse. She had managed to convince herself that she was not at fault for anything that happened when her children were young.

"Then he sexually abused all of you," she replied in a flat voice. Jean asked how mother had been apprised of the situation and she stated, still in the same monotone, "One of the kids at school called me to say that he had been told by the social worker and sheriff." Then she hung up the phone.

An hour later Mother called again. This time she was ranting in a high-pitched tone, "If you had kept your damn mouth shut, gone along with your brothers and sister, and not talked to the authorities, this wouldn't have happened. Dad got out one of his pistols and threatened to shoot himself in the head. This mess is all your fault!"

It did penetrate my fear and sadness at the time, but I couldn't be held accountable for my father's sickness, or the fact that it had become public knowledge. First, no one had called and warned me not to talk to the sheriff's officer. Also, no one had even hinted that my secret was shared. Until that day, I had convinced myself that I was the only child my father molested. I was a very naughty little girl of no worth and, therefore, deserving of all the bad things that had happened.

Jean was stunned by her mother's outburst, but she quietly answered, "The social worker suggested I go for counseling."

Jean's mother lost control and screamed into the phone, "Don't you dare go to any counselor. Sweep it under the carpet and leave it there!" She slammed down the phone and Jean was left with a dead receiver in her hand. She, who had always been the scapegoat, was now cast as the dark shadow in the family's history—the town crier of the family **Secret**.

I had taken the blame all of my life and it was going to continue. I thought that it must be true, though I was unclear as to why. My brothers and sister, I thought, had been brainwashed to believe my blame was absolute, and they were a party to mother's insistence that I not seek counseling. In their eyes, I was at fault for airing what I perceived as the family's dirty laundry. To reinforce my part in Mother's sorry state, I was subjected to a constant barrage of words telling me how bad her life was. How she hated her life. She would employ this method each time I tried to tell her how I was feeling, how I had been treated by Dad. Now that I had let out the family Secret in the minds of the family, Mother didn't want to hear anything from me at all, nor did my brothers, sister and father. None of them spoke to me for over a year. Though I was glad our past was out in the open, I was deeply hurt over the rebuff. I stuffed my feelings and pain as usual. After reading an excerpt from **Toxic Parents***, I had a better understanding of why my family behaved as they did: "The only way many victims can survive their early incest trauma is*

*to mount a psychological cover up, pushing these memories so far
beneath conscious awareness that they may not surface for years, if
ever," (Forward 153).*

Two weeks after the secret was aired throughout the school
system, the sheriff's department, social services and Mother,
Father quit drinking after twenty years of alcohol dependency.
His ultimate motives were never expressed, but it would be
realistic to presume that he needed his wits about him in order
to protect himself from legal punishment—to deny any wrong
doing with a clear head.

Jean spent the next three years trying not to think or talk
about the sexual abuse. As long as she went to visit her parents
and continued to receive what they dished out, they were quiet.
If she tried, however, to do anything they did not approve of,
they criticized her. If she acquired a new friend, they made a
point of saying they did not like that person. It was as if the
revealing of the family **Secret** had never happened and they
resumed the roles they had played their entire lives.

Mother's and Father's relationship worsened. Mother
stressed time after time that she hated her husband. There
was nothing left of their marriage. They didn't go anywhere
together; they didn't share a common goal or common
interests. Mother tried to immerse herself in the lives of the
children who did not want her, for whatever reasons.

By 19—, Jean's own marriage was not the best and she knew
it was never going to get better. She continued to repress her
anger, fear, and overall unhappiness. Kay, Jean's daughter, was
beginning to be a problem because of her dependence on Jean.
She was 22 but refused to go out on her own, tied emotionally
to Jean in an unrealistic, cloying way. She demanded her
mother's constant attention and balked whenever Jean wanted
to be alone. Mother and daughter argued incessantly about
Kay's lack of independence. Kay sat in her chair staring out
the window, day after weary day. She had tried college, she had
tried a job, and nothing worked for her.

I could tell Kay had no clue as to what her next move would be. I couldn't stand to see her sitting in her chair and I couldn't understand her state of mind. I was at a loss in regard to telling her, without reproach, that she was wasting her life away. I found myself yelling at her constantly which caused her to yell back that her lack of anything to do was all my fault. If she had a car and a job she wouldn't be sitting all day. I tried reasoning with her. It never worked because neither of us was listening to the other. Each encounter invariably ended in a shouting match. It was a no win situation. My anger had metamorphosed into resentment and hostility toward my own daughter. Shades of Mother?

Kay refused to help with any of the housework or to assist me in any way. She objected to taking care of her own personal needs such as cleaning her room or taking care of the messes she created in the house. One terrible day in November I couldn't tolerate her inactivity anymore. I grabbed her by the shoulders, screaming at her that she had to take responsibility. We couldn't stay locked in the dysfunctional relationship reminiscent of my own childhood. I had not touched Kay like that since she was a small child, but I was so angry I wasn't sure what tactic I would use next. Both of us began to cry, and I knew our living conditions were out of control.

I needed help from Charles, my husband, even if only a sympathetic ear or shoulder to cry on, but when situations became too tough for him to handle, he went out the door. I was angry with him for not supporting me, and the old feelings of abandonment surfaced.

Mother was there one day Kay and I had our altercation. She was quick to chastise me, "Can't you see how upset she is?"

"What about me?" I asked. "I'm upset too."

Don't I count? I thought to myself. I had no one to talk to about what was happening. I remember saying to Charles, "We need to talk about our problem."

"What problem?" he customarily asked.

That triggered my anger and I yelled at him. This scene replayed itself time and again. The church offered no better solution. I was told Kay was acting out and that I should slap her in the face. I knew that remedy was brutal. It wouldn't resolve anything and most assuredly would make matters worse. Talking to Kay was also useless. Seeking solutions from my pastor about my marriage and my problems went nowhere. They were too jaded. I could not discuss the sexual abuse issues of my past.

We needed professional help. On an especially bad confrontation between Kay and me, I called a center named the Ark. I asked if there was any way someone could help me. I told the woman on the other end of the phone line that Kay was handicapped and I could no longer deal with the problems between us. The woman said I should get Kay on SSI. That began another round of struggle with my daughter. She screamed that there was nothing wrong with her. My mother's influence over the years had convinced her that she was perfectly normal, but apply for SSI we did.

The battle between the two of us went straight through April of 19—when Kay received her first SSI check. She was going to the shelter to work and study every day. She didn't want to, but I told her she would have to move out if she didn't. She was 22. We couldn't afford to keep supporting her, nor did we want to. She needed to be independent and I needed peace and quiet. I couldn't tolerate her attitude. Once again I broached the subject of counseling.

She yelled that she didn't need help, and I couldn't make her go. Period. We had tried counseling before at the request of her school and had gotten nowhere. We were unable to make a connection with that counselor and finally quit out of frustration.

My anger was the greatest I could remember, and I knew I was rapidly reaching a breaking point of some kind. Consciously I did not think that Kay's and my problems had anything to do with my past, and it was this in mind that I again sought family counseling. Little did I know that our problems were a smoke screen for all the pent up emotions that had been happening for 46 years. I realized my effect on Kay was detrimental—unhealthy.

That awareness gave me the push I needed to change the course of my future.

It seemed to me that my life had come full circle. I was Cookie the child, trying to be Jean the adult, then Cookie the child. There was nowhere left to go except around in the circle again and again. The same garbage littered the same road; the cycle of sickness remained unbroken, and perpetuated for infinity.

What I consciously perceived as my daughter's problem was, in essence, inherited behavior from many years, and more likely many generations of dysfunctional family existence. So, it was under the guise of seeking help for the problems with my daughter that led me onto the pathway to mental health and the healing process, to travel painfully, yet persistently, toward my safe house and sanity.

It was time for Cookie and Jean (me) to become one.

PART III

CLEANING UP THE CLUTTERED ROAD TO SANITY

Gather ye rosebuds while ye may,
Old Time is still a-flying;
And that same flower that blooms to-day,
To-morrow shall be dying.

—Herrick

MY QUEST FOR
A SAFE HOUSE BEGINS . . .

As I begin this last segment of my story, I am relieved that I have finally been able to openly express the hurt, anger, disappointment, and pain I felt and hid over the past forty years of my life. Not only has writing this book been cathartic, but I truly feel that stories such as mine can be the motivation for others to seek professional counseling regarding family secrets that take away a person's dignity and replaces it with shame and a deep sense of unworthiness.

To seek a counselor was not easy for me. Many times I struggled with the guilt of my past and tried to evade specific areas of emotional pain. My counselors, both Susan Amon and Joan Franz, never wavered in their beliefs in my ability to *dump the garbage* of my past and clear away the litter to an emotionally stable life.

There were times when I wanted to back out of the pursuit for emotional stability because of negativity I received from my parents and siblings, when it was difficult for me to confront a memory, or to admit what part my mother may have played in my feelings of self-loathing. Many mornings I awakened with terrible fear, almost convincing myself that the pain caused by my search for a safe place was not worth the struggle.

Each counseling session was a strain on me—and my husband, for he shared many of my tears and felt much of my bitterness.

Going through the trauma of child abuse is not a solitary affair. The people in my women's group also suffered and lived through similar circumstances. Their stories have been tantamount to my willingness to expose my inner-self, no matter how emotionally painful, for they have shared their pain with me. We help each other over seemingly insurmountable obstacles in our pathways to mental health.

My search for peace is not quite over. It took decades for me to reach the *bottom* of my ability to cope when past and the present seemed to become a single time frame, and I could not distinguish one from the other, such as that day Kay and I fought over domination of my household. My behavior was too reminiscent of my mother's. Even though I was aware of what I didn't like about myself and my life, I did not know how to stop the patterns of behavior so ingrained in my personality.

I do not expect to totally clear away the debris of a lifetime's degradation and shame in a short time. But, I am getting closer to that day when I will feel safe and secure.

What follows in the remaining chapters of this book are the inroads and back roads of my search. Readers perusing this manuscript should note that throughout the text, the time frames of the italicized inserts change with the year in which they were written and coincide with the progress made in counseling. In this final section the italics are no longer used because the past (Cookie) and I (Jean) have discovered that we can coexist and find peace.

We began putting this story together in 19—, less than a year after I began therapy. It was impossible to work for more than a few hours at a time. Lollie (my friend and co-author) had devised a chronological outline that needed *filler*. Each time she asked a question in those early days, either I couldn't remember specific incidents or I withdrew into my protective shell. Writing sessions were as emotionally debilitating as counseling sessions. I would go home feeling totally drained.

As the months merged into years, to some extent it became easier to supply the needed information for our manuscript—depending upon what it was I had to remember. Also, by early 19—, my therapy sessions were becoming less painful. I was able to sit with my counselor for an entire hour without shaking. Indeed, therapy, seeking and finding answers, and letting go of the past were more difficult than I imagined. Is it no wonder I almost gave up?

Fortunately for my sanity, I did not. With each passing month, I was learning more and more about who I was—that I was a victim of horrendous crimes against my emotional, spiritual and physical self. My assessment of what had happened in my past no longer felt surrealistic. I was better able to analyze the emotional impact of my family's involvement and why I reacted in the ways I did. And it has become ever more evident that my greatest obstacle has been, and apparently will continue to be, my biological family.

As with all of life and the passage of time, there have been changes since I began writing this book, not the least of which was the death of my dad in the summer of 19—. In recollection of the part he chose to take in my dysfunction, I begin the final journey of this manuscript.

Weep not for him that dieth,
For he hath ceased from tears,
And a voice to his replieth
Which he hath not heard for years.

—Mrs. Norton

To Father

May He Rest In Peace

Isn't it strange that the death of one person may become the key to freedom for another person? How many times over these tragic years of my past have I wished my father dead, thereby freeing me from a mental prison he helped create? In this imagined freedom, however, I never considered that death would also cheat me out of a plethora of questions that I wanted and needed to resolve with a man who professed to be my father, and who held nothing in life dear to him—at least nothing about which I knew. What happened to that great rush of *freedom* I should have felt when this person died? How would I ever know the truth?

Why was my father the way he was? I suppose we could conjecture until we are exhausted with the varied reasons that cause a man or woman to become a sadist. In my father's case, I learned about mid-way in my therapy, that his own childhood was wrought with terror and debasement. That fact certainly does help one understand that he, like his own children, had been emotionally robbed. He had acquired all the sick skills he needed to become an abusive husband and father, uncontrollably compelled to choose the route he took through life. He, of course, didn't tell me any of the stories I heard. His sister's daughter, on the other hand, didn't suffer from a misguided sense of loyalty to any of us, and it was she who disclosed The Secret of my dad's youth.

Many times I have used the word *bizarre* in reference to my own childhood; I thought it an accurate term to describe the actions of my father and mother. The term cannot justifiably be employed in reference to the terrors my grandparents subjected their children to in their growing up years. My dad's mother was mean beyond the current dictionary definition, for she willingly and apparently without conscience or concern for the young people being destroyed, led her children into sexual trysts with her husband—the biological father. Whenever my grandfather wanted sex and my grandmother wasn't "in the mood," she sent one of her children into his bedroom to perform the sexual services he desired and demanded. How much more evil can a mother be? She committed emotional murder and the bodies of her children still moved, talked and thought even though, internally, they must have felt dead.

What happened in my father's childhood beyond the sexual abuse? Since he didn't hesitate to brutally batter his own children, most likely he suffered the same fate. The patterns of behavior had been established. He simply carried those into his own marriage and parenthood.

Did my father hate me, as my inner child, Cookie, translated because of the abuse perpetrated on me? I don't know. For obvious reasons, I will never know—at least, not on an earthly plane. His death did not free me of this concern. Did he feel emotional pain, or had that been beaten out of him when he was a young boy? Again, I don't know. I can only recall one incident in which all of us witnessed the softer, compassionate side to Dad's personality, when our beloved dog was lost during our trip home from Oregon.

Why wouldn't he ever confide in any of us? I have a better understanding of this lack of communication because of my own unwillingness to disclose the family secret. Changing one's behavior through counseling and disclosure is extremely difficult. The emotional pain goes beyond definition because each of us is different. For my father to have admitted that something was wrong with his behavior, he would have had to divulge what his parents did to him. I will never know for certain. I think he brainwashed himself to believe his rules, to ease his own internal pain and, therefore, to justify his actions in his mind.

Did he ever feel love? Did he even know how? I can no longer ask him. I would like to think that he knew true, unconditional love from someone at some point in his life. It is so sad to think that a person must go through his/her entire life without being loved. My father could have had unconditional love from his children, but he destroyed that since his own depravity didn't allow him the methods necessary to exact love from anyone.

Some of these questions can never be answered. Specific members of the family who could have provided clues are dead. Those who are still alive, such as my mother and my dad's sister, haven't volunteered to help. In fact, my mother refuses to accept my counseling as a viable method of resolving my inner conflict. Why would she want to help if this involved disclosing her role in the drama of my life or hers? That is a very frightening thought to many people, not just my mother.

Unanswered questions aside, I realize that no matter what happened between Father and me, he was *my father* and old teachings die hard: "Honor thy Mother and Father." Even as he lay, sickly and dying in his hospital bed, had he reached out to me, I suspect that I would have responded as a loving daughter, rather than as a vengeful child demanding a confession before her perpetrator's final breath was drawn.

The events leading up to my father's death, and his subsequent demise, firmly convinced me that we could never have unity as a family. What could have been a perfect time to resolve old hurts, forgive each other for being remote, and enter into our respective futures with a sense of belonging was the same old garbage in a new setting: a hospital room.

In March of 19—, my father, who had been feeling sickly for some time, went to the hospital for an angiogram. While the procedure was being performed, he suffered a stroke. My sister called to inform me of this fact, and stated that everything was under control. He needed surgery, but the physicians had decided to wait until Dad was stabilized.

During the next seven days, he seemed stronger. As planned, early the following Wednesday he had bypass surgery and valve replacement. By late that night, he was fully conscious.

I watched his progress, and his actions in the following two weeks. I had seen people who had this type of surgery get up and go within three weeks. My dad was not responding in the same manner. I wondered what was wrong. He seemed so lost. He didn't talk much, but when he did his voice sounded odd. I finally asked one of the nurses what was wrong, telling her that he didn't respond normally. One nurse told me he was catatonic; they would tell me nothing else.

In the succeeding six weeks, I visited once or twice a week—to stand and look at him as he stared out the window. I never got a response. My mother and other family members said that Dad spoke to them. At first, I didn't believe them. Having second thoughts, I thought maybe he just didn't want to talk to me. I wasn't sure as old doubts about my worthiness, or lack thereof, very briefly flickered through my mind.

Dad was in the Intensive Care Unit for some time. One Saturday I went to visit and found my oldest brother in the hospital room with Dad.

As I walked over and stood by Dad's bed, my brother turned to me and said, in an indignant voice, "I love you."

Talk about shock. I had no idea where that had come from, or why, but his next action startled me even more. He came around the bed, twisted my arm behind my back, and said, "You are going to listen to what I have to say."

My surprise quickly turned to anger. I walked out of the room without waiting or wanting to hear what my brother had to say. I had been abused for too many years and I was not allowing it to happen any longer. By the time I arrived home I was livid. I wrote him a letter, warning him to never, ever touch me again without asking.

From that day until Dad died, I was careful when I went to the hospital. I tried to arrange my visits so they did not coincide with the visits of any member of the family. My brother had taken the liberty of abusing me in an intensive care hospital ward, would the rest feel free to do likewise? I could not stand the embarrassment of what hospital personnel might think, and I did not wish to put myself in the pathway of anyone else's abusive behavior, either verbal or physical. Such actions were stupid and inappropriate in any setting. I was amazed with how much my thinking had changed over the course of therapy. The ensuing weeks would prove that counseling had been the only route for my emotional well-being. My family acted out their craziness in ways I would have been unable to handle had I not the security of a therapist on which to depend.

Several weeks later the same brother and I met again in Dad's hospital room. This time he was talking to Dad, telling him what a great father he was. I didn't say a word, nor did I look in his direction.

As during the previous encounter, he spoke to me before I realized he was going to, "What are you thinking?"

I replied, "I don't want to talk about it here. This is not the place." I couldn't tell him what I was thinking no matter where we were. The entire scene was unbelievable to me because my brother had never been civil to our father. They argued, physically fought, and showed no respect toward each other. The fact that my brother concerned himself with my thoughts was even more unreal. He had never asked before.

He must have observed that I was quietly thinking. Rather than take a chance that I would be truthful, he responded furiously, "Gel your ass out of here!"

I silently walked away in tears. I never saw my oldest brother in the hospital again until my father died twelve weeks later.

Three times, while my father was in the hospital, I talked to him. I knew he was going to die and there were some things I wanted to say. I pulled the curtain around us for privacy, not wanting an invasion by Mother, siblings, or hospital employees to interfere with what I needed to do. I know that my father heard me, even though he neither communicated nor looked at me. Each of the three times I felt the pain of my sadness and the heat of my tears as they silently fell down my face. The last time I visited him in private, I read to him what I had written in the solitude of my home:

"Well, here I am again, Dad. I sense that you can hear me even though you are not looking at me. I cared about you, but because of the abuse you dumped on me, I felt as if you didn't care about me. So, at the end of your life, I don't know how I feel—maybe numb. I don't hate you."

On June 24th, my sister called and told me that Daddy was dying and he only had hours to live. I wasn't sure 1 wanted to be with him when he died. I went to a group therapy session, at which time I discussed my choices, deciding not to return to the hospital, but to go on home. At 9:00 that evening, my son called and said, "Mom, I want you to come to the hospital." For his benefit, I returned to the hospital where I stayed until after midnight.

I watched as my dad struggled for breath, thinking each would be his last. But, he lived on. All of his bodily systems were shutting down, but he kept breathing. After I returned home, I expected any moment to get a call telling me Dad had died, but he survived the night.

The next afternoon, Friday, June 25th, my sister called and said, "You had better come. Dad isn't going to make it." Once more I made the trek into the hospital room in which Dad was dying. My mother, sister, and oldest brother were flanked around Dad's bed. I was dumbfounded. They were leaning over Dad's body, continuously telling him what a wonderful father he was, thanking him for all the wonderful things he had done for us. I was so angry and disgusted that I wanted to scream. These people, my family, were so phony—trying to make the *outsiders* think that we were a close-knit and happy unit. If the scene hadn't been so sad, it would have been funny—a comedy of terrors.

I went home that night certain that it would be Dad's last. It was not. Around noon of the following day, my sister called, saying, "Please come if you want to see him alive." Like an instant replay, I found myself repeating the actions of the day before.

All of us were tired and touchy, as if our nerves were constantly being exposed to something electric. My brothers began to argue about religion so I left for awhile. Shortly after I returned to his room, Dad stopped breathing.

I left to inform my husband and children that Dad was dead, but again, he fooled us and began breathing once more. He apparently didn't intend to give up easily. All of his children, some grandchildren, and other family members, were crowded around him, paying him respect. Somehow he must have known and wanted to stay with the living for as long as he was able. He tried for a bit longer, but at 11:50 p.m., he finally succumbed.

I just wanted it all to be over. I had never been present at a death. I had no idea how I was going to feel, or how I was expected to feel. It took a few days for the reality to sink into my soul. This was the death of my perpetrator, the one who had stolen my childhood. I never received what I wanted from my father and death was so final that I knew I never would. There would be no more chances. I also knew that I would be fine, but I wanted desperately to know what he had been thinking in those final days of his life. I truly needed reaffirmation that he understood what he had done, causing so much sadness.

Yes, I do feel cheated, especially when I remember specific events that caused me great emotional pain and my need of freedom from the brutality was great. I remember the sad dreams of the little girl, *Cookie*, whose fantasy spilled forth on an essay she had to write for a college English class. The essay ended: ". . . but she was safe now in the woods with the birds."

That little girl was, of course, me and I remember, very clearly now, that particular incident in my childhood. I remember thinking how lucky the birds were because they were free to come and go as they chose. I, on the other hand, was a prisoner of a madman's aberrant behavior.

Yes. I did dream of the time my father would die, either at the hand of God or at the hand of someone whom he had hurt. I did dream that if he did die I would be free like the birds. I didn't realize that the dream was a lie to myself.

My father died and *I am not free.* After five years of in-depth counseling, I am freer than before, but I am not the bird who flies unencumbered through the blue skies because my dad died before questions were answered—or in some cases, even asked.

I said my good-bye to Dad in a letter, just prior to his death, but he was unable to read my words. I am taking the opportunity at this time and place to express and dedicate those words to the saddest man I have ever known. Perhaps he will sense my farewell from out there where the birds fly, unencumbered. Perhaps in God's realm my father has been freed from his emotional prison.

A Final Farewell

I am sitting here in this dreary hospital watching you, Father. You are in the bed two feet from me. The doctors say you are dying. I look closely at your face. The remnants of the abusive father are gone. All that is left is an old vacant face, a sad face. I'm sad. There is so much more I wished I would have said to you. It is too late now.

Visitors come and go. Some whisper, some just stand and watch, not knowing what to say. One young nurse says, "What a sweet, funny, old man you are." I just nod my head, acknowledging that I hear her.

You have given me so many emotional scars—scars that will always be with me. I'm sure if I could ask you, you would say there were a lot of things you wish you had not done. It is too late now.

At this moment my mind goes back to a cold, foggy day. We all stood along a highway, somewhere between Washington and California. We were staring at the broken rope that at one time was tied to our big, brown dog; he was lost somewhere on the road. Maybe I think of that time because you were so very sad, and we seldom saw you that way.

I wish that somehow I could have made a difference in your life and helped you in some way. I am able to make a difference in my life—for me. You were the only one who could help you. It is too late now. I have always cared.

Good bye, Daddy.

To doubt
is worse than to have lost; And to despair
is but to antedate those miseries
that must fall on us.

—Massinger

THE FIRST STEP

One of the first steps I had to take in my therapy was to get in touch with the person I had been as a youngster, as well as the person who subconsciously spoke to me during those times when I struggled with stressful situations or memories I wished to evade. *Cookie* was the nickname of my childhood and *Cookie* was the name my counselor and I gave to my inner child who still existed when I felt I needed her.

Though 1 disliked the child *Cookie*, 1 discovered during those initial months of counseling that I used her much too often to make an easy transition from the child *Cookie* lo the adult *Jean*. There were times when I pretended, as a child might do, not to understand a direction in which my counselor was leading me. Even today that inner child has a way of inserting herself into my thoughts, and 1 wish that 1 could fall back on childish ways and days and be relieved of certain painful memories. The difference now, as compared to 10 years ago, is that I realize I never had a childhood. I had simply been a child in age and stature. *Cookie* was a personification of sadness, unhappiness, and a creature whose self-esteem was nonexistent, No wonder 1 didn't like her.

I did *need* her, however, in order to get in touch with what she thought and felt, and how she responded to the various stimuli forced upon her. At first, this was a most difficult task. Not only did I dislike *Cookie*, whenever Joan, my counselor, suggested I describe this inner child, I balked. 1 tried to picture what she looked like, but in my mind's eye, she turned her back on me each time I came close to her face. What was going on here? Surely I must recall the physical characteristics of my own self.

Joan and I discussed why this inner child was so elusive whenever I tried to conjure her in my mind. We came to the joint conclusion that she was hiding, as she did then. She was fearful of exposing herself because no one had protected her when she needed it. Why would it be any different now? Obviously, 1 was still hiding many memories from myself out of the same childish fear of being condemned or punished for disclosing the family *Secret*. Dear God, 1 had learned my lessons well.

As counseling progressed, my dislike of *Cookie* lessened. I learned that each of us has an inner child, somewhere way back in the recesses of our minds. Some people may never need that child to ease pain or sadness. Some may have accepted the inner child as being a beneficial part of their continuing emotional and intellectual growth all through life. With me, the inner child was an integral part of my past. She needed to grow up, and she needed my help to reach a plateau of serenity. When I looked at her in this way, similar to how a (real?) mother protects her infant, my own fear of exposure lessened. I began to use my new-found knowledge in a positive manner rather than to feel threatened by *Cookie's* presence. I became me and a representation of me, a friend with whom I could communicate:

Dear Cookie, You came to visit me today. It is Christmas time again. I could tell you were feeling overwhelmed by sadness. I caught you crying at least twice. 1 wanted to take away the sadness and tears. I wanted to tell you all this will pass. I wanted to tell you that as you grow up you will find many people who love you. I know your loss is great, but I love you and I'm proud of you.

With the realization and acceptance of Cookie and what she (I) could do to enhance my mental wellness, the counseling sessions became more and more productive, but oh, so scary. Going backwards into the horror was almost as debasing as the original molestation. Images in my mind overlapped one another to the point that I truly feared my quest for an unlittered road to emotional health would destroy me before the realization of my safe house.

There seemed to be so much garbage in my life, I didn't believe there was a receptacle large enough to hold it all. I desperately needed to dump some of the rubbish before it spilled over in the container of my mind. Joan suggested that 1 write to relieve some of my confusion and anger. I was encouraged to keep a journal, to write to her whenever I felt the need, to write to my parents and siblings (regardless of whether I mailed what 1 wrote), to write to my husband and children, or anyone I chose. These missives, then, would symbolize my garbage cans. I could express, thereby dump, my fragmented and confused thoughts, and ultimately rid myself of the waste products of a very dirty pathway to sanity.

Because therapy sessions generally lasted only an hour, much of what I disclosed to my counselor did not thoroughly saturate my conscious mind until after I left her office. While driving the 40 miles home, bits and pieces of what had transpired began to penetrate. By the time I arrived at the house, I was an emotional mess. Had I told the truth? Did I remember the facts? Did 1 say too much? What would this counselor think of me? Was I a bad person? Did I unknowingly ask for what I received as a child? I could go on and on, page after page, listing the thousands of questions I indulged myself in on that short 40-mile trek from the therapist's office to my front door. It was in the aftermath of those sessions that I needed to confront my thoughts and it was at those times that I was most inclined to write. The fragments of waste became pieces of paper on which unfolded my innermost feelings and concerns. The pieces of paper, in turn, became the foundation of this book.

It felt so good to unload on something as inanimate as paper. The notes and letters that I decided to mail, however, came alive as soon as I dropped them in the mailbox. Then . . . I really punished myself for having the guts to actually send my exposed emotions to the addressee even if the recipient was my therapist. (What if, somehow, the wrong person read the contents?)

What follows are bits and pieces of notes to my therapist over a two year period. If anyone who has survived child abuse were to ask for my advice, without hesitation I would say: "Write, write, and write some more."

Letters to my therapist:

March 19—

Dear Joan,

You told me when you first started counseling me that I could write to you if I wanted. Well . . . here goes.

You asked me if I hated my Father. I don't think I gave you an answer. I feel as if I'm stuck between anger and hate. Sometimes I can't tell the difference between the two.

I have even given myself permission to hate him. It's still not easy to say, "I hate you, Dad, and I hate you for what you did to me and our family."

I think that when I've recovered, I'll be blank. I won't feel anything toward Dad.

It is just as difficult for me to tell people I care about how I really feel. I have told my husband and children that I love them, but there is so much more inside of me I wish that I could say. It just won't come out.

I love my mother, too, but I am afraid of her.

I respect and admire you so much. Before I started counseling last year, I didn't think I liked women any more than I did men. I feel so differently now. Thanks so much.

Love,
Jean

June 19—evening

Dear Joan,

We talked about how I was going to react when my mother died. I said I didn't really know, but this evening sadness welled up inside me. I feel as if my mother is already dead because she is so far out of reach—like she is not here on Earth. You know . . . when someone dies how it hurts because you can't talk to them anymore?

My mother and I never shared anything from our souls. There was some superficial stuff that we can't even share now. It hurts, but I'll get through it just like I did before.

Love,
Jean

July 11, 19—

I really took the bull by the horns this week. You and I talked about whether I thought my dad was still capable of sexual abuse. I said yes. One reason is that he has never gotten any help. He has never asked for help.

That day he had his step-granddaughter in the bathroom, his reason didn't make sense. When I asked him why he had her in there, he said he was teaching her how to operate the lock on the door. This excuse from a known child molester?

I went to talk about Dad's behavior. For me to talk to the girl's stepfather is like holding a stick of unstable dynamite. He doesn't think anything happened. I don't know if he questioned the little girl or not.

So . . . next I went to Dad. I said, "You had the little girl in the bathroom with you. You had better watch your step. With your past you will end up in jail." I felt myself shaking, but if it stops him from hurting other little girls, it was worth it.

Love,
Jean

Fall 19—

Dear Joan,

When I started thinking about writing this letter, I thought I might keep it—just writing it helped. But, I felt I had to send it.

I'm still feeling a huge amount of anger. I don't understand why, after more than a year in counseling, all of a sudden when I was with you last time, the anger came up like a flood. It made me feel as if I was drowning. That anger scares me. I know I won't survive if I don I let it go, but it hurts so much.

I want to be a whole person. I want to be the person I was meant to be. I know that I am heading that way, but it's so hard.

Love,
Jean

February 19—

To Joan,

Yesterday as I sat with this really neat group, 1 cried, "Help me, my terrible loss to recoup." I was asking that my youth be replayed, with changes, so I could be Cookie again—only loved the second time around.

I listened and wondered if I'd ever be strong enough to accept the reality, I know that if I ask today, they'll probably say, "You are wrong, Jean. You are tough as the rest and you are a survivor of your past."

I'm so glad that I am a part of this special group. They already have a place in my heart.

Love,
Jean

March 19—

Joan,

I was thinking about our talk yesterday. I know why I would rather feel hate or anger toward my mother and father. To me, love means being subservient. I looked up the word in the dictionary and it means very obedient, eager to please, too polite, slavish. Can I love my parents and still be my own person?

I am afraid of that kind of lover, I have been there and I never want to go back. How can 1 say that I love them and not feel a chill up my spine?

Jean

July 25, 19—

Today I started to think about my sister. The tears came into my eyes. I don't understand what's happening to me. After all, she told someone one time that she didn't know who 1 was. So . . . why am I crying over a sister I never had?

I know that she would never read a letter from me, so I'm writing it to you.

Jean

September 19—

Dear Joan,

The anger that I felt come up from deep within my being during our talk today is making me feel very uncomfortable. I think we should go back to it the next time we meet. The way that I'm feeling must have a lot to do with the sexual abuse.

I don't respect Dad. I'm sure that without the abuse, Dad's lack of education wouldn't have mattered as much. But, I have not been able to separate the two—the uneducated man who is my father, and the abuser who is my father.

The feelings 1 have about him as a person are: He is my lather, the part of the reason I am alive, who worked to put food on the table and . . . the person who physically and emotionally beat me in the head, raped me, took away my childhood.

The uneducated man who supported us is my father, and the abusive madman who violated me is my father. There is no way I can separate them.

Jean

My letters to Joan ended abruptly at that juncture in my therapy. 1 had already been a part of the Women's Therapeutic Group since the beginning of 19—and my focus had transferred itself from the singularity of a counselor, to the plurality of a group of people who were considered counterparts. The transition into a group setting, however, wasn't easy.

If I thought it had been difficult and painful to open up to a therapist, 1 found that doing likewise to a group of women was pure torture. What I did do for about six months was clam up. 1 couldn't force myself to look into the eyes of strangers. I couldn't trust their motives for wanting to know about me. 1 feared they would judge me, talk about me, and verbally abuse me. In essence, I internalized every nuance, all body movement, each word spoken as being directed at me. 'That was the depth of my shame.

Because I was blinded by my own sadness, I could not see the sadness of the other women in the therapy group. Because I had been emotionally scarred by the crimes perpetrated against me, I didn't suspect the open wounds that festered in all of us. I convinced myself that I was different, that my problems could never be related to nor understand by a single woman in that gathering of lost souls because they weren't nearly as lost as I. How deluded we can become when our emotional dysfunction supersedes our compassion and empathy for those whose lot in life is equally as dysfunctional. Such was my sorry state when I first entered group therapy.

Looking back, I am so gratified that the self-imposed obstacles of group therapy did not prevent me from overcoming the obstacles of my past. 1 had taken that first frightening, tenuous, step. In a metaphorical sense, I could fly—above the guilt and shame, beyond the bitterness. I could look down upon that littered highway of my past and see the safety of wellness far off into the distance, even though parts of the road were shrouded in fog and other sections caked with dirt.

The sensations I began to feel were scary, yet emotionally intoxicating.

I might never be completely free of my past sadness. I was becoming an outsider to it—not a prisoner because of it. I can validate the old truism: "The first step is the hardest."

> Narrowness of mind is often the cause of obstinacy;
> we do not easily believe beyond what we can see.
>
> —La Rouchfoucauld

OBSTACLES

Self-Imposed

As we all know, regardless of one's state, be it normal or abnormal, life has a way of putting up roadblocks as we journey from childhood, to adulthood, and then to whatever may be awaiting us just prior to and after death. For what I shall refer to as normal people, the obstacles are surmountable (though some are painful, such as the death of a loved one). This may be due to a remarkably healthy support system of family and friends, an unwavering faith in the basic goodness of humanity, an unbiased belief in a higher power, and a strong sense of purpose or beneficence.

One of my primary reasons for counseling involved learning how to sweep garbage to the wayside of the road to mental wellness, as I chipped away each painful happening until it no longer controlled me. All of this had to be done without guilt—a tall order for someone whose every decision was guilt-ridden because she feared she was a bad person. I wanted desperately to be like those normal people described above. Then I would find happiness. Oh, yes, my goals were monumental, commendable and unrealistic. I discovered, in short order I might add, that I could not simply pick up each piece of abuse perpetrated upon me and toss it carelessly into a trash can. Very hard work was necessary. Susan, the counselor with whom I initially began therapy, suggested I keep a journal of daily happenings, memories of the past, feelings of anxiety, and to list obstacles as they presented themselves. The suggestion, itself, seemed to be an obstacle. Everything was an obstacle. Without too much hesitation, however, I tackled the directive and began keeping a journal. I decided it couldn't really hurt, it might even help, and in retrospect, I am thankful that I followed through. Several of the entries are sprinkled throughout this chapter primarily to help me eliminate some of those obstacles.

For many of us who are what I shall refer to as abnormal because of emotional dysfunctions, the obstacles are overwhelming, overpowering, and controlling. We see life as a constant battle. We find evil in many things and many people within our immediate society. Some of us may look to outside forces to supply us with happiness, rather than to look within ourselves for contentment. Others hide inside themselves so they will not be easy prey for further maiming of their delicate hold on sanity. In other words, we possess a seemingly innate ability to provide ourselves with many, many, of our own obstacles. I was very adept at building those roadblocks. From my very first memory, I fought battles. At the young age of 18 months, I was forced into battle by my father's sexual deviance. I didn't realize that I was fighting back, but I was by internalizing my pain. As I grew into pubescence, after suffering at the hands of both Mother and Father, I battled with shame. I mentally fought with myself about the part I must have played in my parents' abuse: I was a bad girl; I was imperfect; I was ugly; I was stupid. Adulthood provided more battles on a daily basis as I worked very hard to not become like my parents.

Journal entries:

Fall 19—

I want to get rid of all this anger. I am madder at Dad and Mom than anyone else in the world. Sometimes just saying it helps.

January 19—

I talked to Susan today about Mom and Dad. In so doing, I could feel the pain in my stomach. One of these days I will be rid of all the pain and anger. It is a terrible feeling. They will not change. I will change and take control of my life.

Same day

I want to be my own person. The only way I can accomplish this is to make a break from my mom and dad. Maybe this will help get rid of some of my pain. My dad hasn't spoken to me in almost two weeks, just because I was too busy to talk to him on the phone. He got his anger up, he can get it down.

Same month

I went to see Susan today. She is really a big help in sorting out my feelings. I am so angry with Mom and Dad. They wouldn't let me show anger when I was a kid. Now I feel like a bomb about to explode. I don't know how to disarm the bomb without hurting myself.

September 27, 19—

This is my mother and father's 49ᵗʰ wedding anniversary. I went to find them a card. I had no luck at all. It is really terrible trying to find a card for people who don't like each other. I have learned in the two years of counseling that I don't have to do things for my parents, just because they are my parents. I should do it because I want to. I have a choice—a free feeling I have never known.

May 19—

In the last few weeks I have realized something. I'm not obsessing over the sexual abuse any more. I know that I was just a little girl and not responsible. I know that no matter what I do or say to my parents (or about them), they are not going to change. When I look at them now, I see sad people. I still think a lot about what I'm doing—taking care of myself. That is something I was never allowed to do either.

Same day

Another issue that presented itself today is my feeling that the people who do care about me are going to abandon me, turn away, or maybe they will even die and leave me alone. I feel as if my parents abandoned me when I was a child. The feeling is the same.

Same month

Another mental picture that always arrives unbidden when I'm with my biological family is the one of the skinny, little girl, trying to make her father and mother proud of her.

Finding evil in all men was no problem either. My father had me almost convinced that the world consisted of mean, deviant men, who used their children as non-thinking, non-feeling, playthings. Men were allowed to drink, carouse, dominate, subjugate women, torture animals, and defile babies. They could use whatever means necessary to have their way, which included manipulating the *Bible*'s goodness by turning God's words into something evil and fearful.

Journal entries—backtracking:

Fall 19—

I was really angry with Dad today. When he gets me on the phone and I don't feel like talking to him, he refuses to hang up. I wish that I could tell him just how I feel, but he won't listen. I stamped my feet and screamed when I got off the phone. I felt better. Doesn't he know how boring he is? Sometimes I can't stand to look at him.

Same time of year—Different day

Dad, you hurt me. All I want to do is get rid of all this pain and be a normal person. I feel like screaming. Sometimes I put my head under a pillow and do just that.

May 19—

I see him (Father) shooting a cat right in front of my eyes. This happened when I was about six. I have never forgotten the incident because of what it told me about my dad. I remember being terribly scared. The cat flew into the air and died.

Same month

I picture a man (Dad) who is mean to his children. He called me names. When I stop to think about him, I think mean.

I don't believe that I consciously looked for evil in my mother in those early years. In the back of my mind there was always a glimmer of hope that she would come to my rescue as did all story book mothers. It was later when I was a teenager that I began to suspect she was not my ministering angel—the savior of my soul and "anointer" of my sadness. Was she, too, evil? I am still having difficulty with this question because of all the poems and stories written about the goodness of mothers. Yes, I have been programmed to believe the myth and this is one area in which I do not wish to find evil, yet I am again reminded of Dr. Forward's words in **Toxic Parents**: ". . . the mother who is told of the molestation by her children but does nothing about it. When this happens the victim is doubly betrayed" (158). Still, I did not want to find evil in my mother, but my relationship with her did facilitate my ability to find evil in other women.

Journal entries:

Summer 19—backtracking

I had a dream. In the dream my mother was telling me how simple I was. She has told me in real life that I am simple. I would say to her, "What you see is what you get." This time, in the dream, I told her, "There is a lot more to me than you know." I was standing by a pile of lumber and as I stacked it, I said, "See, you didn't know this and that was hidden in here." When I was finished, I had stacked all those boards in a nice neat stack, nothing was hidden any more.

Fall 19—

I'm so angry with you, Mother. Why do you do this to me? I dreamed that I sat you down in the big white chair that Susan has in her office. I threw pillows at you. Why don't you love me like a normal mother would?

Same time of year—different day

I'm so angry with my mom today. She uses my daughter to tell me she is mad at me. She says I've pulled into my own little world where she cannot go. So what? Maybe I want it this way. I'm so tired of the pain. I wish that I could talk to Susan. I wish my daughter was not used by Mother. God, life hurts.

Same time of year—different day

I'm mad at you, Mom. You didn't keep me from being hurt. You were told but you didn't listen (Ames 219). Why didn't you listen? Why did I have to cry alone all those years?

May 19—

Sometimes I want Mother's approval—something I never received from her. At other times I don't care.

Same day

I have stopped trying to control my mother. I know now that's what I have been trying to do. I know my letters, phone calls—not even my withdrawal—is going to force her to face this nasty picture. I'm sure mother and I are doing the same thing. Both of us think that if we hold out long enough, the other will come on bended knee, saying how sorry she is about all the shit that happened. I have no doubt that it will not happen on her part or mine. I believe I have lost that glimmer of hope. That little glimmer made me miserable anyway.

October 19—

I never want to be like my mother. Most of the time I have to baby her along or agree with her, or she will get mad and take off walking down the road.

May 19—

On Saturday before Mother's Day, I took Mother out to lunch. I hugged her. She didn't hug me back and I really wanted her to. One of my women's group members asked me if my mother had ever hugged me. I answered no. I was then asked, "Then why do you think she would be able to hug you now?"

May 24, 19—

Yesterday was my birthday—number 49. I don't feel bad about being 49. What I have trouble with is all the pain I had getting here. I spent 15 years pushing all the pain down into my soul—even further than the depth of my soul. Doing that made me physically sick and mentally ill. Mother's attitude has not helped me at all. When I was 46 I decided I was at the bottom—I couldn't feel any worse and it was time to start the climb up and into the sunlight of sanity.

June 19—

I went to the coast this weekend'—all by myself. My husband and I have been bound to each other like glue for so many years that I needed to know if I could do something independent of him. My mother fussed and griped. She was upset that I would do such a thing and rather than be happy for me, she complained about my independence: "You mean you're going without a man? If you break down you would need a man with you."

Most definitely, once I met and married my husband, I looked outside myself for happiness. I had not been able to find happiness from within, locked securely inside the emotionally dysfunctional prison of shame, guilt, self-doubt and self-loathing. Surely my husband would put the salve of love and kindness on my festering sadness, thereby taking away the pain. What a shock it was when I came to the realization that Charles was unwittingly a student of my father's manipulative courses in Parenting and Expected Behavior of Wives.

Journal entries—backtracking:

Fall 19—

Today was not so great. In fact, it was awful. Charles loves me, but I don't know if he can take the pressure. He folds up emotionally, then I end up supporting him and forgetting about what I need.

December 19—

I'm not very happy with myself tonight. I let Kay and Charles upset me earlier today. Usually I know what to do to stop them when they "gang up" on me to fight a decision I made, but I didn't see their attempt to control me until after the fact. Charles said he didn't understand why I was so insistent about our daughter moving to her own place. Kay stood next to her dad, looking dejected and hurt. They made a formidable pair. Feelings of guilt crept into my resolve, but anger won and I stood my ground. I was upset with both of them and myself for allowing the situation to control me. There was a time I would "stuff" everything. Now I let myself cry.

May 19—

Today Charles and I talked about some feelings I know are true, but I hate to tell anyone. I need attention. When I was a child the only time I received any caring was when I was sick. Now I am an adult and it is the same way. On the one hand, I want to be emotionally well. On the other, I want to be cared for in the same way as when I was sick. I can't seem to separate the two without wondering whether my feelings are healthy or stuck back in my childhood when I needed nurturing. I internalized my anger rather than act-out on that anger as many emotionally dysfunctional people do. In no way am I condemning those who do act out because I have a first-hand understanding of their reasons. I sincerely believe that I internalized the anger because I was scared to death of the outside world. I never chose alcohol to anesthetize my rage because someone might witness my drunkenness. Promiscuity never entered my mind as either a mask for my fury, or as a punishment against men. My reputation as being a good girl would be sullied and if the family or church learned of my behavior I would be devastated. I didn't run away. Where would I run to? I did not get into physical altercations as a child or adult because I truly did not want anyone to notice me and my unhappiness. They might think I was not normal or they might want to know why I was unhappy and I could, under no circumstances, reveal the family secret.

Journal entries—backtracking: Fall 19—

I feel as if I've been abandoned, just like when I was a little girl. The people who are supposed to care about me—my biological family—are going away one at a time. They are not physically leaving me. They still live in this town. Spiritually and emotionally, one by one, they are rejecting me. I am sure it is because the more I am able to accept and deal with my past, the more my family fears the truth will be revealed. I, too, am scared of the truth. Sometimes I think I continue in therapy to prove how wrong my family is, that they are to blame for all of my present troubles. If I point this out to them they will learn and love me because of their guilt.

Different day

I don't know why I continue in this line of thought when I know better. Can't I say to myself, "Jean you are an adult. Stop. It's grow-up time. Let Cookie go, let her become part of the adult that she needs to be." This child in me continues to beat at the world that hurt her. This is like swinging at the wind. It does no good.

January 19—

I don't understand what's happening to me. My thoughts tumble one on top of the other as I keep trying to find a reason for the abusive behavior of my mother and my father. What did I do wrong to cause them to treat me so badly? Some day I will feel better about myself, I think.

May 19—

Will I always be this hurt little girl Cookie? I want so much more out of life than what I got. Was it my fault? Maybe I feel like two different people because the child in me still has not had her childhood, and the adult in me knows that the storybook childhood not only didn't exist, it never will. Intellectually I know the difference between Cookie and Jean. Emotionally they share the same mindset and are locked in a stalemate.

February 13, 19—

The last few months have been a struggle. It seems that I continue to wrestle with some heavy duty stuff: guilt over money spent on therapy; guilt about Kay and whether I should have made her move out; worry about being sued because I exposed the secret; and concern about my biological family and if I'm being fair. I have spoken to others who have been abused as children and their fears mirror my own. Guilt is a major obstacle to most of us. If we can get beyond the feelings of guilt, we have a good chance of progressing to emotional stability.

Sometimes I think an issue is dead and buried, and up it comes again—bigger than ever. I thought my inability to trust was not a problem anymore, but it is. I am damn mad at the people who abused my trust and hurt me in such a way that I can never be the way I was meant to be—normal. My mother and father hurt me almost beyond repair. My husband also damaged our marriage. He is so sorry about that pain he caused, but it will never be the same. Because of our pasts, inability to trust is another area we abuse survivors share.

April 15, 19—

I'm still feeling that stupid feeling when I put myself in a position where I am not in control, at least not yet. My parents, siblings, and husband are very adept at saying something that causes me to react as they want, not as I really feel. I met my mother at Del Taco, outside at the picnic tables. I told her what I was doing in regard to counseling, and why I had sought help. I knew what her response would be yet I had agreed to meet her anyway. I put myself physically and emotionally at her disposal—to be hurt. She said, "I don't have to hear what you say. A lot of this crap is just your imagination. I'm not going to sit here and listen." She left. There I was, alone and feeling really stupid. I hope I don't allow that to happen again. Sometimes I still feel so very sad. I know there are people who love me. My husband and children love me, as well as my friend and my counselor. Why couldn't my mommy and daddy love me?

May 19—

I am just getting through a very tough month. Charles and I have had a difficult time communicating with each other. We went backwards emotionally and allowed the inner child in each of us to try and control what was taking place. Neither of us was being very mature, demanding that one give in to the other. I had trouble with my biological family. They are trying to frighten me into giving up therapy.

June 9, 19—

I'm very lonely. Yes, the self-imposed obstacles were virtual mountains blocking my emotional health, but the day that I walked into Susan Amon's (my initial therapist's) office and asked for help, was the day I began chipping away those mountains. I wasn't sure what I expected as we began to talk. I didn't know what was expected of me. I was scared without understanding just what it was I feared, other than the repercussions of my parents when they found out I was being counseled. I thought I needed an instant, painless cure for my unhappiness, and I wanted a counselor to relieve me of the dread that I was already emotionally defeated.

Needless to say, I didn't receive an instant, painless cure for what ailed me. Tearing down self-imposed obstacles is not only an in-depth, slow process, it's excruciatingly painful giving up something one has become used to possessing—even if it is detrimental to one's mental health.

As therapy progressed, the obstacles were torn down and thrown into the dump heap where they belonged. At least, those that I had imposed upon myself. I was finding more peace within myself, more serenity without guilt—and more aggravation from my family.

The first and worst of all frauds is to cheat oneself.
All sin is easy after that.

—Bailey

OBSTACLES

Familial

November 19—

My oldest brother called today, asking if he could go to
my counselor with me. How long has it been since The Secret
was exposed? In the fall of 1982? Dear God! Twelve years have
passed—five and a half since I began counseling. All that time
I wondered if anyone in the family would acknowledge that
what I endured was the truth—what they suffered was true. I
have prayed that we could be a real family, that we could learn
to share our lives and our ups and downs. My brother's call
verified that my prayers had been answered.

I called Joan, my counselor, and an appointment was
established for January 17, 19_. I was so happy and excited
with the realization that my brother had truly made the first
move, that I called my friend, the co-author of this book. I
imagined that the ending of this manuscript would take a
much different turn than what we had originally planned. It
is truly difficult to put into words the feelings and thoughts
that went through my mind. I found myself wishing the time
would pass quickly. I pictured the scene in Joan's office, my
brother on one side of the desk, with me on the other. We
were a bit uncomfortable because we hadn't seen much of
each other since Father's death, but Joan helped us to feel at

ease. What a wonderful picture this presented. I should have known, however, that my imagination and hopeful dreaming neglected to consider one very important fact. My family is not normal. None of its members behave in a mature, responsible manner when it comes to emotional behavior. "Because we live and grow in relationships to others, especially our families, our problem behaviors often can be understood as our responses to others and as our attempts to influence them" (Myers 501).

January 2, 19—

I was disappointed today when I called my brother to confirm the day and time of our appointment with Joan.

"Hi," I began when he answered the phone earlier this evening, "I just wanted to remind you that our appointment with Joan is on the 17th of this month at 3:00."

"We-1-1-1 . . . My sweetheart is coming in that day," he responded quietly.

"Can I make the appointment for another day?" I asked, almost shyly, fearing his negative response.

"Nah." There. He did it.

"Are you canceling completely?" I said, certain of the answer.

"Yes."

I thanked him politely and ended a conversation that was between the strangers we were, are, and will be.

January 3, 19—

My daughter came by today. She and my mother have maintained a good relationship in spite of all the garbage strewn on my road to mental health. I didn't expect it to be any other way—it is very important that family ties be kept. I have never taught my children to dislike my family, only to be wary of my father's record of molestation and to avoid the negative emotional traps that guided my parents through their lives. I believe in this way I prevented the abusive behavior from perpetuating itself beyond my generation, at least for my children and grandchildren. "Being ill-treated when young seems to predispose people to abuse their own children by repeating the pattern of their own experience" (Clayman 262).

Kay, who was with my mother earlier, was apprised of my call to my sibling and his subsequent cancellation of our joint counseling meeting. In her usual innocence she repeated Mother's latest conversation with her. She said that Mother told her my brother had only offered to go with me to counseling in order to discover what I had been telling the therapist over the past five years. He wanted to authenticate his version of the truth, then report back to the family. I was not surprised by this revelation. It sounded like something he was quite capable of planning and executing.

Five years ago, before I began my long journey to a Safe House, I would have been devastated by my brother's actions. Today I have only to go through my letters and journal files to be reminded that some are very adept at fooling themselves, and pretending to believe the half-truths and lies supplied by mother and father. He no more believed the fiction than I, but he was working very hard to convince himself that he had not suffered the same fate when we were children.

My brother was not alone in his self-deception. My other siblings determined that what I was doing, through counseling, and now through this book, was detrimental to the family, that all of what I discovered about myself, what I remembered fully, and what I had suppressed, were figments of my over-active imagination—an emotionally sick need for attention and sympathy. How I wish that were so. Not to have lived through my childhood would have been sheer joy, but I did.

During the process of therapy, I learned that it is not uncommon for the victims of abuse to protect their perpetrators

(Forward 153). It is so much easier to deny bad things, and focus only on what the outside world saw and believed to be the truth. There are many reasons for this. In our family, we had been conditioned from birth that the family's secrets belonged only to the family. To make family business public knowledge was a punishable offense by the family.

For years I believed the fallacy also. Had my sanity not been at stake, I would still be an active member of a fictional family. Instead, I chose to expose, express, and exorcise. As I traveled the littered highway to my present serenity, I tried very hard to include the family in the wellness process. All my efforts as can be read below, seem to be of little avail. I can only hope that I have planted the seeds of reality in the minds of my siblings (in particular), thereby helping them understand the necessity and beauty of expunging the garbage from one's soul.

July 19—

To Mother:

I don't need your approval either. I'm doing this (learning to drive) for me—no one else. I am driving that truck as part of my recovery from abuse. I feel better about myself. I wanted you to be happy with me and my accomplishments, but you're not. I have a good support group. They are very happy for me and my new skill.

I get so tired of you telling things to Kay. It puts her in the middle. She loves us both. I know you will probably tear this up, but it's the truth.

Jean

September 19—

Dear Mother,

I regret I could not come to dinner, but I felt as if I was being pressured into something that was going to make me miserable. The atmosphere in your house is too thick with distrust and sadness. The people there say they love me, but I don't think they even like me. If you really cared about my feelings, you would want the best for me, even if it hurt you.

All my life I put other people ahead of me, but I'm not doing that now. Sometime in my life I have to think about me and love me the way I needed to be loved. I am not taking the blame anymore for the way you treated me. I was just a little kid and you were supposed to be an adult.

You said I was nuts in the head. If there are any crazy people in this family, it's not me. I'm the one going for help; everyone else has his/her head in the sand.

*I want to be my own person—to be free of all the craziness that I grew up with. I pray someday you will get some help for yourself. I care about you. Don't forget that. You may tear this up and throw it in the trash if you choose—that's your business (*I think as I write, the words will remain in my mother's mind*).*

Sincerely,
Jean

December 6, 19—

Hello Mom,

This might possibly be the last time I write to you in this way as you don't seem to really care about my feelings anyway.

You really blew it—our relationship—and I've had it up to my eyebrows! You had a chance to go with me to the counselor and at least have your say in this matter. If my son or daughter said that I hurt them and they wanted me to go to a counselor with them, I would go as fast as I could. By your refusing to go with me shows me that you don't care. (In reality what it represents is fear.)

I am slowly allowing other people into my life—people who care about me and my emotional welfare. I guess they will take the place of my lost family—the ones I cried so many tears over the last 18 months. Maybe now I can go on and be the person I was meant to be.

Bye, bye,
Jean

April 19—

I'm angry with you, mother, because you called me names and beat me. You stole my childhood and now I have to go through a lot more pain to try to fix me the way I should be. Your love was always so conditional. If I was a good kid and did what you told me, you loved me, but if I tried to tell you how I felt, you withdrew your love. I have wasted so much time trying to understand your motives for treating me the way you did. Indeed, this inspired much confusion in me when I was a child, and I cannot honestly say that I think any differently as an adult.

May 23, 19—

Dad,

I need to talk to you, but since I can't, I'll do it this way (audio tape). I'm thinking about our birthday. I'm thinking about 48 birthdays, during most of which I was a sad and angry person. I was the scapegoat in your family. When someone got picked on, it always seemed to be me. All I ever wanted was a father to love me in a normal way.

You stole my childhood. I feel as if I always knew about sex, so you plundered my innocence, too. You took all the fun out of being a child. I turned into a person who was afraid of everything.

I was your first child, born on your birthday and named after you. I wish that I could have been that special child I was meant to be, as all children are meant to be. You know what I found out? I am a special adult. I can do more than I ever thought possible.

I'm not writing this to try and change you. I am changing. I'm not even writing this to make you happy or sad. I'm doing it for me. We all have choices to make. You made yours. Now I'm learning to make my own and one of those is to confront you with what you did to me. The sexual abuse you put me through never completely leaves me, but I'm learning how to deal with what happened.

I hope you have a nice birthday.

Jean

Late June 19—

Mother,

Sometimes when I see you, I feel like screaming at you. I'm still holding onto so much anger because you continue to blame me for what happened when I was a child. You continue to tell Kay all about it. It is the kids' fault if they get beat up—they asked for it. Right? Damn it, Mom, I wish you would leave my daughter out of this. Stop telling her it's all my fault that you lost your temper and beat me up. Mother, you know what

*I want from you is to be able to sit down with you and Joan
so that we can talk to each other without blaming. I would
like to be accepted as the person I am, and not what you wish
I was.*

July 1, 19—

From Mother to me

*Jean, I wish only and always the best in life for you and
that in the months to come you will begin to realize, more
than ever, that God is your only source of happiness and
contentment*

Love, Mother

July 3, 19—

From Mother to me

*Jean, just a word. I feel that letters and phone calls only
come to a stalemate. If you want to call here for a pleasant
chat, fine, but no more discussions on problems. I won't do it
anymore and please do not send me any more letters. I will not
open them and they will come flying back to you. I must put a
stop to this continual unhappy barrage of words. Useless it is.*

*Probably at this stage of the game we would have a lot of
differences. I am willing to talk with you about nice, happy
things, but no more unhappy talks. I have my own set of
difficulties these days that I am trying to cope with, so please,
just don't hang any letters on me, or unhappy phone calls. I
don't need these things—now or ever.—**MOTHER**—(Her
usage of uppercase letters!)*

July 11, 19—

Letter to Mother—never mailed, given to counselor

I received your letter last Friday. It made me feel sad. I accept the limits you have set. This is your privilege to do that. You are taking care of yourself. You are doing what you think is best for you.

Do you really know what you are doing? I care so much about you. I wanted us to take down the walls between us. You say it hurts too much. I can't remove them alone, however, and sometimes I think you just don't like me. That has hurt more than you know. I can't take down the walls without your help; I can't make you love me.

There are some things that I can do alone. I can make sure I don't have any walls between my children and me. I can love me for the person I am. I can do things that make me feel good about myself without fear of guilt or shame.

You have set the new boundaries so I will have no contact with you at all. As I write this, I feel a load off my back. I've been hitting myself against those invisible walls that won't move. I can stop now. I'm sure it will hurt less.

Jean

August 19—

Dear Mother,

It is too bad I couldn't come to your party. I agonized all year over this. I didn't feel as if I could even say "Happy Fifty Years" when I knew how bad your marriage actually was.

You tell me that the Welcome Mat is out. When you found out I was writing a book, you told me I was no longer a member of your family. This is the first time you have said I could come back. I'm still writing the book. I have been told *it is super. I have never told you that you weren't welcome in my home, but you never come here. I have wanted us to be friends and, at least, talk about the problem. You want me to pretend the past didn't happen, but I cannot, and I will never pretend again.*

There was a short period of time in my life when you were there for me. From 1984 through 1989 we shared a common interest in our search of the family tree. Genealogy brought us together. The rest of the time I suffered in silence—all alone. Now, you will not give in one inch to help. I have given all my life. Your children loved you so much. All we wanted to do was protect you from the bad stuff that Dad was doing. All I want from you now is to be able to talk to you with Joan Franz present to help us sort out this garbage. Then we can go forward into a more comfortable and peaceful future.

Jean

So much for family unity. As my co-author and I reread this particular chapter, we injudiciously laugh at the folly people create in their minds—then try desperately to convince others that the folly is nonfiction. Five years ago I would have been hurt by the words of my siblings, believing every bad thing they said about me. I would have listened to the words of the Scripture they spouted under fear of exposure, then tried to apply those passages to my life—regardless of what doing so would have done to my emotional well-being.

I do not mean to make light of their fear today. It is real. I subjugated myself to that same fear for over forty years. The difference between them and those of us who seek help through counseling is that we can no longer live with the hidden guilt and shame without eventually going mad. The perpetuation of The Secret had to be broken if at all possible.

I do not want my children, or their children, to suffer as I have.

> Understanding is a well-spring of life unto him
> who hath it: but the instruction of fools is folly.

> —Proverbs 16:22

Open Letters To
My Mom—And Myself

It is my fervent wish that my mother reaches the same Safe House in which I now reside, and that she finds peace within herself . . . before she dies as my father did. If my father had found even a semblance of sanity before his demise, or wanted to let us know he was saddened by the part he played in our dysfunctional family, none of us knew for he couldn't talk those final hours of his life. My mother still has the power of speech, good mind, and the freedom of choice that God has given each of His children. May she use all those factors with wisdom.

Because I feel so strongly about the benefit of counseling, and because I truly do love my family in spite of all that has happened over these many years past, I wish to part with words that I hope will inspire, as well as ease their minds as to my reasons for writing this book. My intention was not to attack anyone in the sense that I allowed hate to dominate my motives. Nor have I wanted to expose The Family Secret for monetary gain or revenge. I do not have to justify this manuscript in any way. I do feel, however, that many may benefit and learn that each of us must do what is necessary to find internal happiness—for we cannot find it without. We cannot expect our pasts to disappear for they have shaped each of us into what we are today. We may repress all the bad stuff, but we cannot escape the bad stuff. It is part of our heritage, just as our relatives are. We can change ourselves with a conscious, painful effort to use the past as a learning tool, a ladder on which we can climb to the top of our potential if we so desire.

Those of us who have suffered at the hands of an abuser can learn to understand that we were victims and, therefore, not guilty. We can eliminate much of the litter from the highways of our past—those cleaner roads, then, can lead us toward an emotionally stable future.

Even my family can benefit. After all, it is a matter of choice, is it not?

A final approach

My first wish for my family is happiness because we have never had enough.

My second wish would be love—someone to love and be loved by, for everyone needs love.

My third wish would be health so that we can live out the remainder of our lives doing what we want to do.

Finally, I wish that all of us could be friends—having loving mother/daughter, sisters/brothers, relationships. I love all of you.

Jean

Dear Jean,

This last letter is written to me—Jean. I have talked about what I wish for my brothers and sisters, now I want to talk about what I wish for myself. I wish that I could love myself and others without being judgmental. I wish that I could help others learn to accept themselves as people of value.

I wish to let go of the past, yet remember that what happened to me cannot be changed. My future can be whatever I choose it to be.

I want to be—always—a loving wife, mother, and grandmother. I now have the capabilities necessary to make this happen.

I wish that if I live fifty more years that they be happy and fulfilling.

I love you,

Jean.

EPILOGUE

Jean,

I remember when I talked to you the first time on the phone. You let me know you had a good therapist and wouldn't change unless you had to. It had taken you a long time to trust her and since she was closing her practice, you had no choice but to trust her recommendation. You must have said trust five times in our short conversation. When I saw you, you didn't meet my eyes. In fact, you appeared as a daisy does when it is deprived of water—beautiful, yet droopy, head down, hiding.

You began to reach out, to trust. As you did, your self-esteem began to blossom and grow. Then it was time for you to join Group. For the first few months you did a wonderful chameleon-like job of disappearing. However, reaching out, a baby-step at a time, you began to reclaim, first Cookie, then the teenage Jean, the young woman, and finally to the adult you are now. I watch you now in group and in life—speaking out, disagreeing, laughing openly, trusting forthrightly.

I feel privileged to have watched you grow—from getting your first driver's license, to going back to college. Thank you, Jean, for allowing me to walk beside you for a moment.

Love,
Joan C. Franz, M.S., M.F.C.C.

Addendum

In May of 1995, 1 felt as if I had come to a stand-still in my therapy. My counselor suggested that I attend an intensive four-day workshop.

The speaker was a man by the name of Terry Kellogg. The first night's lecture on co-dependency was comical and informative. I discovered that some of my relationships were dependent—even though I had never thought of them as being so.

The next morning we went to another lecture where I learned that addictions were more than alcohol and drugs. I am addicted to my feelings.

After the lecture we were separated into groups of seven. In my group there were five men and two women. This was a surprise. I was sure I didn't want to be in a group of men. I didn't view men as sensitive and open. I thought that only women had a handle on these things. I was very wrong. The men who were in my group cried and expressed their feelings openly.

The group leader was also a man who was able to express an entire range of feelings. I had never seen men do this. Furthermore, I was amazed that these men could show anger, sadness and joy.

In the four days that we were there, we changed. During our first session, one man sat in the corner with personal objects around him like a shield: a briefcase sitting on the floor at his side, a jacket hanging on his chair, and a brown bag that appeared stuffed with other personal items sitting in at his feet. When our four-days of meetings were over, that man had moved his things to the side. He discovered he didn't need to protect himself. Likewise, I had taken my "special" blanket and learned that I did not need it.

I am so glad that I went to the workshop. Prior to attending, I didn't know that my therapy would end in September. The workshop was a booster shot to keep a sense of direction toward my Safe House.

I have spent six years in therapy. I would not trade those years for anything. Even though it was difficult and painful, and there were times I wanted to quit and push the past back onto that littered roadway, therapy was worth every moment. I learned that I have a choice to be Cookie, the little girl, or Jean the confident woman. No problem. I choose Jean.

POSTSCRIPT

My father died on June 20, 1993. He had written a living will about five years before he died. After his death, my mother and sister rewrote the will excluding my daughter who was to inherit their house upon Mother's death. My mother may have wanted the house to sell for her own profit. Mother died August 30, 2005, after which my sister found out the second will was not legal. Kay was awarded the house in 2006.

Until her final days, Mother continued to deny the family's dysfunction, convincing herself that she had done the best she could raising her family. Perhaps in her mind, she had.

WORKS CITED

Ames, Louise Bates, Ph.D. "Child Molesting." The *Ann Landers Encyclopedia* AtoZ Garden City, New York: Doubleday & Company, Inc. 1978, Vol. I and II.

Clayman, Charles B., MD, Medical Editor. The American Medical Association. *Home Medical Encyclopedia.* New York: Random House, 1989; Vol. IA-H.

Donaldson, Mary Ann. "Incest Years After." Pamphlet Forward, Susan, Ph.D. **Toxic Parents**. New York: Bantam Books, 1989. "Hidden Victims." *Psychology Today*. Sept/Oct 1992.

Kemeny, Margaret, Ph.D. Quote from: Bill Moyers Healing and The Mind. New York: Doubleday, 1995.

Lerner, Rokelle. Affirmations For The Inner Child. Deerfield Beach, FL: Healt Communications, Inc.

Miller, Deborah, Ph.D. and pat Kelly. *Coping With Incest*. New York: The Rosen Publishing Group, 1992.

Myers, David G. *Psychology*. Hope College, Holland, Michigan: Worth Publishing, Inc. 1989.

Spock, Benjamin, M.D. *Decent and Indecent: Our Personal and Political Behavior*. New York: McCall Publishing Company, 1969.

The Bible. King James Version.

Treasury of Familiar Quotations. New York: Avenal Books, 1974.

Worlets, Janet. *Healing Your Sexual Self.*

Author Bio

Margaret Morris is retired, having worked with the severely handicapped at the elementary grade level. After living 47 years in a state of limbo due to excessive sexual, physical, and spiritual abuse by her father, she sought and received counseling. She also returned to college, received her driver's license, and became employed outside the home. Her story is one of courage and a desire to understand why families become dysfunctional. Remarkably, Ms. Morris is neither bitter nor filled with hate. She tells her story in order to help others reveal family secrets that eat away at the core of productivity and happiness.